WHAT'S DRIVING YOU???

HOW I OVERCAME ABUSE AND LEARNED TO LEAD IN THE NBA

PUBLISHED BY TRIMARK PRESS, INC., DEERFIELD BEACH, FLORIDA.

LIBRARY OF CONGRESS CATALOGING-IN-PUBLICATION DATA

WHAT'S DRIVING YOU??? HOW I OVERCAME ABUSE AND LEARNED TO LEAD IN THE NBA
KEYON L. DOOLING
WITH JOEL AND LISA CANFIELD

P. CM.

ISBN: 978-0-9767528-9-9
LIBRARY OF CONGRESS CONTROL NUMBER: 2014940981

G14
10 9 8 7 6 5 4 3 2 1
FIRST EDITION
PRINTED AND BOUND IN THE UNITED STATES OF AMERICA

COVER DESIGN AND ILLUSTRATIONS BY JAMIL JIRON
COVER PHOTOGRAPHS BY DAVID I. MUIR (WWW.DAVIDIMUIR.COM)
IMAGES CAPTURED AT MOMENT 2 REMEMBER STUDIO IN SUNRISE, FLORIDA

A PUBLICATION OF TRIMARK PRESS, INC.
368 SOUTH MILITARY TRAIL
DEERFIELD BEACH, FL 33442
800.889.0693
WWW.TRIMARKPRESS.COM

WHAT'S DRIVING YOU???

HOW I OVERCAME ABUSE AND LEARNED TO LEAD IN THE NBA

KEYON L. DOOLING

trimarkpress
DEERFIELD BEACH, FL
800·889·0693

DEDICATION

THIS BOOK IS DEDICATED to my wife, Tosha.

When I was recovering from my breakdown, I just wanted to be held—and she was there to do the holding. I will forever admire her strength, her grace, her poise, her tone when she speaks, her smile, her eyes, her compassion, her love, her toughness, her grit, and her selflessness. She is the very essence of a woman and I love her dearly.

There are three people in our relationship: God, me, and her. I want this union to last another forty years, fifty years, even a hundred years.

And with His blessing, we will make it that far.

PREFACE

PREGAME NOTES

"WHAT'S DRIVING YOU?"

During my thirteen-year career as an NBA player, I became famous across the league for challenging my teammates with that very question. The reason I asked it was
simple: I believe that when you tap into your core desires
and motivations, when you keep your ultimate goals top-of-
mind, you will achieve at the highest level you're capable of.

"What's driving you?"

The scary thing was, I never fully dealt with my own answer to that question until it was almost too late. I didn't
consider the fact that demons that stay hidden just grow
stronger if you don't root them out—and I had a big one
lurking inside me my entire playing career: Around the
age of seven, I was sexually molested. And it took me almost
twenty-five years to deal with how that incident had affected
me emotionally.

"What's driving you?"

What's driving me now? I want everyone reading this book to understand how abuse affects its victims—especially when they keep it bottled up inside like I did instead of getting therapy. In my case, it caused me to have a complete and very public mental breakdown when that old wound was unexpectedly reopened—and it's why I spent the early part of my second season with the Boston Celtics in a psychiatric hospital instead of on the court.

"What's driving you?"

What's driving me is the desire to finally tell the truth—the whole truth—for the first time publicly in this book.

Yes, this book is about what happened to me as a kid and the resulting long-term damage that followed me into adulthood. But it's more than that. It's about what it takes to attain your wildest dreams—in my case, making it to the NBA—and then finding out that's just the start of your battles.

Don't get me wrong; my years in the league were awesome. But nothing comes easy, especially when your goals are huge. My journey from the hood to the NBA involved unrelenting pressure from those who needed me to succeed, enormous obstacles I had to overcome at almost every turn, and unexpected challenges that forced me to readjust my attitudes, expand my knowledge, and improve my skills. It also forged my character and taught me so many valuable lessons that a thousand books couldn't contain them. I put the most important ones in here.

Finally, this book is about recognizing the dark places in your life and giving them their due. If you don't, they will eventually overcome you—because you've left yourself open to them. It's like playing a bball game when your team can't deliver on defense—you're going to get outpointed every time.

I was vulnerable to my own personal darkness. But with the help of God and those who love me, I prevailed and found a new beginning. I am blessed to be able to share my story with you.

In order to tell that story, however, there are names and details I won't mention, for the sake of friends, family members, and the community I grew up in. I will be transparent, but I can't tell everything, because there are people that I know and love; I have to think about their well-being. I want to see them get the same opportunity to heal that I got.

Make no mistake, though, this will be a very candid account from my perspective. I know from my own journey, that after you've gone through dark times, your light shines even brighter. The pain you've endured turns into a passion to help others who are still struggling. That's why I'm not ashamed to share what happened to me—because I want to help prevent it from happening to others.

I've been blessed with incredible success, and I want to share those stories. But I also want every young person reading this book to know it doesn't matter who you are or where you come from—you can find your own personal success if you're willing to work hard, maintain your focus, and keep your passion alive.

Thank you for taking the time to read my story. May God bless you in your life journey.

THE BREAKDOWN: PART ONE

SEATTLE

I WAS ON THE BOTTOM FLOOR of a mental hospital. Or, more accurately, I was in hell.

In this mental hospital, which proclaimed itself as the "#1 Hospital for Psychiatry," being on the bottom floor meant they considered you one of the most messed-up patients in the facility. As they did the paperwork on me, I heard the other patients yelling and moaning like they were completely out of their minds. A lot of them were. It felt like a bad horror movie, a movie where I was going to be the next victim. Granted, I was having problems at the time—but the bottom floor? ME?

Please, God, no.

True enough, I was in the middle of a full-blown freak-out. I was paranoid and schizophrenic. I started yelling, "Get me out of here! PLEASE!" I didn't feel human anymore. I felt like a caged animal—the lowest of the low.

The really sad part was, just a few weeks earlier, I was on an amazing high.

1

I had trained really hard for my second season with the Boston Celtics. The team had been very competitive the season before—we made it to Game 7 of the Eastern Conference Finals. I wanted to do my part to help us get even further—so I had bulked up to 208 pounds. It was the biggest I'd been in eight seasons, and the new weight was all muscle. I was in the best shape of my life, which is what I aimed for— because I loved my team and couldn't wait to get back.

But, since I wasn't due back in Boston for a couple of weeks, I was doing something I considered equally important. For the past few summers, I had been doing some charity work as the ambassador for The GameTyme Foundation, which was founded by my friend, J. Johnson. I was in Seattle doing an event with my then-Celtics teammate Avery Bradley in the community he was from. The thing people don't understand about NBA players is that many of us come from humble beginnings and we're anxious to give back any way we can to the places we're from.

The GameTyme events were becoming bigger and bigger and more and more popular. Businesses sponsored these events, where we spoke to young guys in rough neighborhoods and showed them how to lead in their communities as well as forge connections with other communities. We also delivered much-needed supplies to underprivileged families. The basic idea was to nourish the minds, bodies, and spirits of these kids any way we could—and, being NBA players, we knew our presence alone would have a big impact on them.

That day's event was awesome—and I was ready for my reward. Our tradition was to eat at a great restaurant after one of these engagements. When I was in Seattle, my pick was always the same—the prime rib at the Metropolitan Grill. I love prime rib and eating it always reminds me of my dad, who had passed away a few years earlier. We didn't have it all that often, but when we did get to a nice steakhouse, he would always rub his hands together and say, "Oh, I'm getting that prime rib tonight!" When I order it now, I feel a little more connected to my Pop.

My friends and I went to the Metropolitan feeling good. We had accomplished a lot and I looked forward to a delicious meal with them. We got a table, I ate my prime rib, excellent as always, and then I had to go to the restroom.

That's when the trouble started.

I went in the men's room and there was one other guy in there, white, about six feet, two inches tall, weighing around 240 pounds. A big guy. And it seemed to me like he was a little drunk. I didn't know how else to explain the fact that he was using more than one urinal at a time— I hadn't really seen anybody do *that* before. But this guy was lurching from one to another, making a big mess as he continued to do his business.

I knew if I tried to use one of those urinals, his business was going to get all over me. Suddenly, I felt on edge. I remember thinking to myself, "I'd better use the stall, because if he pees on me, I'm going to have to put my hands on him." So I went into the stall, but left the door open.

As I stood there peeing, I suddenly felt something I most definitely did not want to feel...a hand grabbing my backside.

I looked back over my shoulder. It was the drunk guy.

3

I wasn't done with *my* business, so I kept my eye on him the whole time. When I finally finished, I turned around and got myself together, and, almost all in one motion, I CLAPPED my hands in front of his face and then spread them apart real, real wide, so they were on either side of his head.

My eyes were burning as I said as fiercely as I had in me, *"Do you know that I can kill you right now, with my bare hands?"*

That got his attention. Then I got to the real question. The question that was the most important to me.

"What is it in me you see that you feel you can do this to me???"

At this point, he was scared. He tried to calm me down. "Dude," he said, "I'm just kidding, I do that with all my friends."

I yelled back, "NO! *I'm not your f—ing friend!"*

God, forgive me for my language but that's just where I was.

I went on. "Who do you think you are? Who do you think you are that you can treat me like that? What makes me so inferior to you that you can treat me as a man like that?" I repeated, *"Do you know I can kill you right now with my bare hands?"*

Still overwhelmed with anger, I left him there, walked out, and sat back down at my table. I ordered dessert—a chocolate soufflé—thinking it might make me feel better. But as I told my story to everybody at the table and saw their shocked expressions as they heard what had happened, I felt a powerful rage growing inside me.

I had felt that kind of rage before. When I saw movies with The Incredible Hulk, I could identify with Bruce Banner having an anger so great that it could literally transform him into a monster—and having absolutely no control over that anger. That was in me, even though I was never sure *why* it was in me.

My dessert came and I ordered a glass of red wine, hoping *that* would calm me down. I was trying to cool down. I couldn't.

I kept trying to talk myself down from it. I had walked away from the "dude" in the restroom, because I said to myself that I *needed* to walk away, out of respect for the people who were donating their hard-earned money and time to the charity I was representing, out of respect for my affiliation with the NBA, and ultimately, to protect my family and my livelihood. If I did anything crazy, I could lose everything I had worked so hard for since I was five years old. I knew I had to walk away without anything else happening.

But there I was, at the table with my wine and my dessert, and the anger's still building, building and building. We finished eating, paid the check, and headed for the door. I figured the best thing I could do at that point was to go enjoy Seattle. See the beautiful views, take a walk through the hills, get a good look at the water, calm myself down, and go back to my hotel room.

I walked out of the restaurant with my friends with that plan in my head, but there he was. The guy. Just sitting there outside of the restaurant.

Bruce Banner became the Hulk.

I basically blacked out—I couldn't control myself. I just remember grabbing him and picking him up in the air off the sidewalk.

As I held him there, I grabbed him by the windpipe. I wanted to kill him, to be honest. The Hulk was in charge and I felt like an unstoppable beast. I don't remember ever feeling like that before, so charged with negative energy.

I don't know what would have happened if one of my buddies, somebody who paid his own way to fly out and support GameTyme, hadn't arrived at just that moment. He had missed his flight to Seattle, so he was late meeting us at the restaurant. In the second he was getting out of the cab, he saw me choking the guy and he moved fast to pull me off him.

The dude got out of there fast, as you would expect. That didn't make me feel any better. I was left with that horrible anger still burning inside me.

My mother was in Seattle with me, so I went to her hotel room and told her what happened that night. She was as confused as I was by my strong reaction, and so rattled by the state I was in, she insisted on praying for me.

But the anger was still burning.

My buddy, the one who had stopped me from choking the guy, stayed in my room that night to watch over me. He was worried about me too—with good reason. The demons weren't out of me yet. Yeah, I'm sure the word "demons" sounds a little crazy to some of you, but I actually felt as though I was in a battle with something bad and out to get me.

I couldn't sleep, I was tossing and turning, and my mind was flooded with weird, dark flashbacks that I desperately wanted to go away. Flashbacks of gunshots I saw when I was a child. My Pop in his casket at his funeral. Lots of other hurtful, disturbing images that were all coming at me at once—especially from the time when I was molested as a kid.

After all those years of pushing them down, the memories started coming back and wouldn't stop.

At three o'clock in the morning, I decided to go for a walk outside to try to lose the rage. I practiced breathing techniques to calm myself down—when that didn't do the trick, I tried calling on the Lord to help me. Nothing was working. Finally, I called my wife, Natosha (she was back in Florida and probably still asleep) and told her about what happened at the restaurant that night. I still hadn't told her about what happened to me when I was a child. I had no words for that.

After talking with Tosha for awhile, I started to feel more relaxed. She prayed with me and told me everything would be all right. A little ray of light started growing inside me then thanks to her.

Still, I couldn't hide what was happening from myself. An emotional vault that had been locked inside me for years had unexpectedly opened. The extreme anger I was experiencing brought up a whole lot of other feelings I hadn't allowed myself to acknowledge since childhood.

Feelings that would take me to the bottom floor.

HOME COURT

TO UNDERSTAND ME, you have to understand where I come from.

In my case, that place is Fort Lauderdale, Florida. Now, when you say "Fort Lauderdale" to most people, they think of drunk teenagers partying hard on the beach during Spring Break—that's what everybody across America saw back in old corny 60s movies, up till today on MTV Spring Break specials.

Well, I grew up only about five miles inland from that beach—but it might as well have been a whole world away.

The area I grew up in was, and is, predominantly black. Even though the original black settlers of Florida fought side by side with white soldiers in the US Army and worked to build the railroads and establish the farms that originally helped Florida grow and develop, segregation became more and more of a fact of life throughout the South in the early 1900s—and Fort Lauderdale was no exception.

That meant black families were suddenly banned from living near the beach that would become so famous in later years. Some already had been living there; they were forced to move inland. A boundary had been set— and black people were told they could only reside *west* of the railroad tracks that ran north to south through the city. Yes, folks from my neighborhood were allowed to work in beachfront homes—but working there was all they could do. And when it came to actually enjoying the surf and sand, they could only go to the designated "Negro" beach, which you could only reach by ferry until a road was finally built in 1965.

Now, it's easy to become bitter about these harsh historical realities. But I feel blessed that my faith has always shown me that the good always co-exists with the bad. Sure, segregation kept us out of the more prosperous neighborhoods, areas that had a lot more resources and economic opportunity—but it also caused our neighborhood to become a thriving, tightly knit community whose bonds are still strong to this day—despite the many difficult challenges it has faced for decades.

To build that community, however, some crucial needs had to be met. Because of segregation, essential services were suddenly out of reach to the generations that came before me—and ways had to be found to provide those services within these new boundaries.

In 1922, the black Fort Lauderdale community was blessed by the arrival of Dr. James Sistrunk, a gifted surgeon who was not allowed to operate on patients in white hospitals. Instead, he devoted himself to providing the only real medical care the new neighborhood could count on. He established his own practice and, in 1938, he helped establish its first medical facility, Provident Hospital (which is now the Mizell Center, located just a few blocks from my old childhood home).

Dr. Sistrunk helped save the lives of many people who were just too poor to pay for his help—and when he passed in 1966, Northwest Sixth Street in my neighborhood was renamed Sistrunk Boulevard in his honor. As a matter of fact, the whole area itself began to be referred to as the Sistrunk District.

A community, of course, also needs to educate its children—and, two years after Dr. Sistrunk set up shop, that need was met when the Dillard Colored School opened its doors. At first, it was just an elementary school, but later on, it became a high school, the *only* high school for black kids in Fort Lauderdale up until the 1950s. That's the high school I graduated from—but it almost wasn't. Why? You'll find out about the hard decision I had to make a little later on.

Yes, health and educational resources were important, but the community also needed to build businesses that would help support its families and allow the area to grow and prosper. I'm proud to say that's where my grandfather made his own vital contribution.

The original Leroy Dooling (my father was Leroy Dooling Jr., and my brother is Leroy Dooling III) was a vital part of sparking the growth of Buning the Florist, a Fort Lauderdale business. He was the first man hired by Arthur Stone, a white man who had bought the original store on a whim in 1945. My granddad helped the business grow to eleven stores that were bringing in a combined $6 million a year when Mr. Stone sold the business in 1999.

My grandfather didn't share in any of those profits; that, again, is just the way it was back then. But he was a gifted entrepreneur and he paved the way for my father to find his own success. My father grew up working for Buning's alongside his father. He learned firsthand how the flower business worked—but, instead of seeing all the profits go to others, he was determined to realize the benefits of building his own business for himself—and for his family.

Which is why, in 1967, my dad opened Leroy's Florists. My grandfather was all for it—and allowed my father to use his home as collateral so he could qualify for the loan he needed to get started. Leroy's became the first black-owned floral business in all of Fort Lauderdale.

My Pop (actually, he was everyone's "Pop"—that was what everybody in the neighborhood called him) was smart about the business. He struck up a deal with a local funeral parlor and put his store right next to it. Obviously, funerals needed flowers—and Pop was there to provide them.

Leroy's Florists became a very successful venture—part of a thriving group of black-owned businesses on Sistrunk Boulevard. You'd find liquor stores, pharmacies, restaurants, doctors, lawyers, a hat shop, and markets like the Bass Brothers and Mr. Willy Walker's grocery store, which is still there to this day.

It was the Rodeo Drive of the hood.

Many of those businesses did well and my father's was no exception. Yeah, the area had its share of drug dealers and prostitution, not to mention blocks of public housing projects for the families that couldn't afford homes of their own. But, in the main part of town, the community was on the upswing—and that was the environment I was born into on May 8, 1980. At that time, the Doolings were a respected and prosperous bunch; it was a great family to be a part of.

I was the baby boy of four kids; my mother, Brenda Dooling, had my oldest brother, Eric, twelve years before me. Leroy III was born six years before me and my sister, Tameka, five years before. The six of us all lived in our home at 2016 Northwest Third Court, right by the north fork of the New River; my father bought the home himself and paid it off within eight years. He was enormously proud of that and rightfully so.

For seven or so years, it was pretty much an idyllic childhood—until I walked through a door I never should have gone through. I had no warning that I was approaching that darkness, however—I was too busy having fun.

SMALL BALL

PEOPLE ALWAYS ASK ME HOW I first started to develop my basketball skills. And they always give me a funny look when I tell them where that happened.

It was in the bathtub.

Yep, I had a little hoop at one end of the tub and I'd try to sink the perfect shot with my kid-sized basketball. You didn't have to nag me into taking a bath—I loved it.

The fact is I grew up in a sports house. Pop, my older brothers, and me—we all loved football and basketball. But our lives were far from being all fun and games. Pop worked a lot, and I mean, a *lot;* he not only had the floral business to run, but he also had a cleaning business going for awhile. That meant we worked a lot too. We all pitched in to help both companies be as profitable as possible— even if it killed us!

That's an exaggeration of course, but, once, I came close. I remember when I was around five or six years old, I was helping my mom clean a downtown office, when I saw a dish of candy on somebody's desk. Well, hello! I quickly helped myself to a piece—a little too quickly, because it immediately got stuck in my windpipe. Lucky for me, my mom saw I was choking and BOM-BOM, she did the Heimlich maneuver on me and popped that piece of candy right back out of my mouth. Didn't stop me from grabbing some more later on, though—that's what being a kid is all about.

So yeah, we were a hardworking family—but we played hard too, and my Pop always had time to support his boys when they played sports. Pop had been a very good athlete when he was young, but unfortunately, because he had to work for his dad and also started a family of his own right out of high school, he had too many responsibilities to be able to pursue any kind of career in pro sports— so he poured his passion for athletics into us.

And we were more than willing to share in his enthusiasm. The standard was set by my oldest brother, Eric. Eric was incredible as a basketball player. He was extremely talented, but, as in my Pop's case, the timing wasn't good. In the 80s, it was all about football in the South Florida area, so his opportunity to go to a big-time Division I School wasn't there—but he still went to college and set a good example for us and a lot of other kids in the hood.

I was in only first grade when he started at Bethune-Cookman University in Daytona Beach, a historically black college, but I know I felt a lot of pride at being able to go watch him play college ball. Unfortunately, he had knee injuries and some other physical problems that kept him from reaching his full potential—but his inspiration was a blessing to me.

WHAT'S DRIVING YOU???

I grew up loving a lot of legendary players—guys like Michael Jordan, Isaiah Thomas, Magic Johnson, and Larry Bird—but if you ask me who really taught me what basketball was all about, my answer would be Eric. He taught me how to use my body the right way, how to look at the game and, maybe most importantly, how to *think* the game. Don't get me wrong—my other brother and my Pop were definitely in the mix when it came to coaching me on the basics that helped me develop my skills, but Eric took it to a whole other level.

Just like a real coach, we'd watch tapes over and over and analyze plays. Now, I'm not talking about tapes of *my* performance on the court, I'm talking about big games we'd tape off TV, like the Final Four. I was only five, but I remember watching the '85 Final Four where Patrick Ewing dominated (he would later be ranked as the 16th best college basketball player of all time by ESPN). Eric would stop and reverse the tape on certain plays and teach me what was behind what was going on. Understanding the mental aspect of any sport is crucial— and he gave me that enormous gift when it came to basketball.

Even though I was twelve years younger, we had a strong but very competitive relationship—we each tried to win out over the other, whether it was video games or push-ups or sports. Naturally, I was usually on the losing end because I was so much younger, but there comes a time when the student catches up with the teacher. That time came when I was a teenager and Eric was in his twenties. I beat him for the first time in a basketball game—and man, that did not go over well. It ended up being not only the first time

17

I came out on top on the court, it was also the first time I came out on top in a fight with him! But overall, he's always been a great big brother and has been very supportive throughout my life, despite the big gap in our ages.

After Eric went off to school, my other brother, Leroy, stepped right in and took me under his wing. I went with him when he played basketball on other neighborhood courts and he let me play with him and his friends and continued that education Eric had started with me. We also had the same kind of awesome competitive relationship as I did with Eric; our constant video game contests stoked the fire in my belly to WIN, a fire that kept on burning and helped me achieve on the court.

The truth is all my older siblings schooled me, knowingly and unknowingly. Being the youngest, I was able to watch them go through all the important life transitions that awaited me, and I could see what was involved in them. Work, relationships, high school, and college—I saw what they went through and learned from their experiences. That's the benefit of being the youngest.

The real schooling, especially when I was little, came from my mom, however. And it didn't stop at teaching me my ABCs either. I learned all the basics from her because she spent the time to make sure I did. She nourished my mind and spirit as no one else did at that time; she's the one who took me to the library to make sure I read and took me to church to make sure I knew the Lord.

But I didn't just learn what life was all about from my family; the community as a whole was also there to teach me. I know that it takes a village to raise a child, because mine most definitely helped raise me. It was a great place to be a kid, for the most part. Within a few square miles were all my relatives and friends, not to mention the family church, basketball courts, and parks where I loved to play.

I never lacked anybody to play with either.

I grew up in a very active neighborhood and there were children all around, many of them my age. In the summer, an average day for me was to wake up, grab my ball, and dribble it all the way down to the basketball court at North Fork Elementary, which was only a few blocks away. Somebody looking out the window at me might have just seen a little kid bouncing his basketball down the sidewalk, but in my head, there was a lot more than that going on. I was imagining I was in the last NBA game I watched on TV, dribbling around people, even dribbling *through* people, pretending I was Michael Jordan or Isaiah Thomas or another one of the then-current NBA greats I loved to see perform.

The park by that elementary school is where I grew up, where I shaped myself. And I wasn't just playing basketball. As a matter of fact, back then I probably played more football than anything else, because I was good at that too. And what was really great for my athletic development was that I got to play against older kids—and I got to test myself against them. That forced me to push myself beyond what was normal for my age and continue to improve my skills. I mean, from the beginning, I was playing on full-sized courts. No kiddie stuff for me—at least after I got out of the bathtub!

Still, I never thought I would be the one to go on to the

NBA. When you're the littlest kid in the family, you think it's your big brothers who are going to end up going pro, not you. Me, I just loved to play and I loved the game—but I wasn't going to be the big dog on the court. It wasn't about me at that time. I thought it was all about them, because I looked up to them and thought nobody was better.

But they saw something in me. They knew I was going to be good at a very early age and they always told me I was going to be better than them. That made them push me hard to reach my potential—but that was okay. They had a good balance of looking out for me and being tough on me.

So yeah, I loved basketball, but I also just loved to be active and use my imagination when I was a kid. That's why I was so happy to be able to go to Walker Elementary instead of North Fork Elementary, the school that was actually closest to me. Walker was about a mile away from our house, but it was worth the walk. It was a magnet school, focused on performing arts, so we would learn drama, music, dance, and great stuff like that; it had better opportunities as well as better academics.

Because I had to make that walk, I connected more and more with my community and my relatives. I would walk home through what was then the Dixie Court projects and stop at the store house there every day, where my friends and I would get a pickled egg, hot sausage, or something like that for a snack. I had an aunt and some cousins who lived in that area, so I was always cool with that walk. A lot of days, I would stop at my aunt's house and hang out— she was at a point in her life where she was taking care of a lot of family members. For example, we had an uncle who was not quite right in the head. He had to live out back in a hut, because sometimes you never knew what he was going to do. Some days he actually thought he was Jackie Robinson!

Later, I began going to the Boys and Girls Club after school—it was just a few blocks away from Walker. I was more than ready—I was incredibly jealous of the older kids who got to go there and couldn't wait to get in myself; it was a safe haven and a place where you could learn a lot of life skills you might not find out about in regular school. I also hung out a little at the local YMCA, where I first took boxing and a little karate too—but it wasn't as cool so I didn't go there all the time.

I really learned how to fight at the Boys and Girls Club, but I also had my mind expanded there. They had programs to teach you about voting, safe sex, and other important lessons every kid should be taught. A lot of my personality was formed there and it was also the place where I played on one of my very first basketball teams. While some other kids had a very different experience, I have nothing but happy memories at that club.

The very first basketball team I played for was at the place where I'd play for my very *last* neighborhood team; Dillard High School. Eric was playing for the Dillard Panthers at the time and they had a recreation team for kids my age. I was five when I joined. My position was the same as it always would be—guard. And that was the first inkling that I had that I was good, very good, at the game of basketball. I was better than everybody—heck, I thought I was Michael Jordan!

Playing for that team became my first real bonding experience with teammates I loved and respected. Of course, I could not imagine at that point the ordeal I would go through with one of those very same teammates.

VIOLATION

IT'S OCTOBER 24, 2013, and I'm sitting in my SUV bawling my eyes out.

Because I'm parked about a football field away from where something unthinkable happened more than twenty-five years ago—and I'm reliving the moment that's haunted me ever since.

When it came time to write this book, I knew this chapter would be one of the most difficult. That's why I felt it was necessary for me now, as an adult, to go back to the place where I was molested. I wanted to go back with a pure heart to reflect on what happened and why—and to also hopefully finally release the pain that was buried inside me for so many years.

Hopefully, you can tell from the preceding chapters that I had an awesome childhood, growing up in a family and a community where I felt loved, encouraged, and protected. That all helped form the man I am today.

But, as I said before, I believe good always co-exists with

bad—and, when I was around seven years old, the bad side showed its face in an unforgettable way. It left an imprint on my unconscious that threatened to destroy not only my career and my family, but my life.

Why did it take until well into my manhood to face what happened when I was around seven years old? Because I did not feel that I was free to acknowledge this incident and others when I was a child. Now, that's nobody's fault. That's just how it was. People didn't talk about that stuff then and it's not that much better now, even in the age of the Oprah tell-all interview. The huge Penn State-Jerry Sandusky scandal proves that adults who should know better still don't and those who are responsible for caring for children too often abuse that powerful position.

For example, take another very recent and large scandal that hit a lot closer to home. In February of 2012, a former counselor back at the Boys and Girls Club that I had belonged to as a kid was arrested for allegedly molesting dozens of children in my old neighborhood, beginning around 1995. Now, that was after my time there and I never had anything but good experiences at that club. But I grieve for those innocent kids who were lured back to this guy's home and taken advantage of.

My point is, I'm far from the only kid who was ever victimized in this way—and that this kind of incident, especially when it's not addressed in a meaningful way soon after it occurs, can have far-reaching, negative repercussions. Yes, I have a lengthy and successful NBA career I'm proud of, and yes, I now have my own awesome and loving family, but even with all those incredible, amazing positives, the events of that horrible day decades ago couldn't be erased. Instead, they stayed in my unconscious brain like a ticking time bomb.

And when that bomb finally exploded, it threatened to blow apart my entire world.

That's why I feel it's important to share the full truth of what happened to me that day. For the first time publicly, I'm about to do just that—and I do it for all the other victims who endured an experience like mine. It's nothing to be ashamed of, because *it isn't your fault*. It took me a long time to come to grips with that simple fact.

It was starting to rain.

Since it was a typical summer day, I was heading to the courts at the elementary school down at the end of the street. Me and my best buddy at the time, a teammate on the Dillard High recreational team I played on, were going to play a little. He was just as good as me at that point in our lives and he was like my right-hand man on the court. We had a strong friendship and did everything together at that time.

But, as we got close to the courts, it didn't seem like the rain was going to let up.

I had about two bucks on me and I said to my buddy, "Man, let's go to the store house and get a soda and hot sausage." The store house was on the other side of the projects next to the school, so we went there, got our goodies, and were walking back toward the school, back through the projects adjacent to the basketball court.

It was raining harder. I heard a friend of my brother Leroy's calling to us from his doorway. I turned toward him and he said, "Ya'll come in here, it's raining too hard out there."

I knew the guy, because, as I said, he hung out with my brother and his buddies. So I didn't think twice about it. Why would I? He always seemed pretty cool. He was a big kid and six or seven years older than me. I wasn't so big at the age of seven. I was pretty average-sized until middle school when I had a growth spurt. And I was probably feeling good about an older kid like that wanting to hang out with me and my friend.

Nobody else was home, it was just him and us. It was still raining pretty good, so we just chilled. He started playing some rap music and we took turns doing what we called "rockin' the mic"—which just meant doing your own free-style rap over a song.

We did that for awhile—and then he changed it up big-time. He put some porn on the TV.

Now, this didn't set any alarm bells ringing in my head. Since I did have older brothers, I had seen porn before. It was pretty easy to access either in magazines or on videos. It was something older kids watched, whatever, obviously me and my friend weren't into sex yet. So the three of us just sat there watching the tape.

The video came to the inevitable scene, where the man finally ejaculated. That's when it got really weird—because, at that moment, my brother's friend turned to us and said, "Yeah, know what? I can do that too."

He said he wanted to show us how it happened. And that's when he made us do things to him to get him off.

After that, I just remember running out. Just getting out

as fast as I could—leaving my friend behind. I didn't care. I just knew I had to get out. It was a visceral reaction.

Was I scared? No. I was mad. And embarrassed that it had happened.

My friend didn't come out of there for a few more minutes. When he finally did, we went back to his house to hang out. Neither of us talked about what happened. I can't even remember if it was still raining when we left or not. To this day, we've never talked about it—which is why I'm leaving his name out of this.

Later that day, I went home and took a shower. And as I took that shower, as I cleaned myself off, a massive anger took hold of me and never let go. From that point in my life, that anger was something I continually struggled with. And when I finally couldn't fight it any longer, when it wouldn't stay down after all those years, the results were devastating.

But, at the time, I felt like I had to keep it down. When you're that young, you really don't have the emotional tools to process sexual molestation. I only knew that I never wanted that kind of thing to happen ever again. I thought I had to be tougher to prevent it. In my mind, only the strong survived—the ones who don't take no mess, who are smart enough to fight their own battles and know enough not to put themselves in certain situations like I had just unknowingly done. The anger motivated me to not only be physically strong, but mentally strong too. And to be prepared to defend myself.

But all of this happened inside of me. Nobody—not my family, not my other friends—could tell anything bad had happened to me. I didn't say anything about it and I did my best to push it down to a place where I didn't have to think about it. But it affected me in many profound ways.

The most obvious change in my outside behavior was that I would never go anywhere without having a knife on me, even though I was still a little kid. Emotionally, I was suddenly questioning my masculinity and sexual orientation. That's not something you usually have to wrestle with at age seven, but, after what had happened, I sure did. I went out of my way to start talking to girls and flirting with them to prove to everyone—mostly myself—that I was straight. I pushed myself into some very bad situations as a result.

Obviously, no matter how hard I tried to pretend it didn't happen, the incident still messed with my head on a daily basis. It was overwhelming, having something like that happen to you and feeling like you couldn't tell anybody, even though there were plenty of people around who loved you and cared about you.

But I was not about to tell any of those people—because I thought I was the one who would look bad, not the guy who did it to me.

My friend, the one who was with me when it happened, he suffered too. The event really, really messed him up— even more than it messed me up, in my opinion, because he suddenly couldn't concentrate, he couldn't trust people and he was, in general, very insecure about himself. Whereas, in a weird way, it caused me to become more and more focused, it affected him the opposite—he grew more and more unfocused. I could see the change—but, again, neither of us felt like we could talk to each other about what had happened. If we could've, it might have helped both of us carry this overwhelming weight.

When you're the victim of this kind of crime at an early age, you often blame yourself for letting it happen. You even think maybe you encouraged it to happen because of something you did. You think, "Why me? What did this guy see about me that caused him to think I would participate in this stuff?" That's what I mean about questioning yourself. Deep down, I would worry about what kind of signals I was sending out that I didn't know about. That anxiety would finally unleash all the anger I was burying, more than two decades later.

From the outside, you'd think I was one lucky kid, and in a lot of ways, you'd be right. My family was well-off at the time, so I had Legos, I had G.I. Joes, and we had all the latest video game systems, like Nintendo, Sega Genesis, Atari. But suddenly, having almost everything a kid would want didn't matter so much. Suddenly, I wasn't a regular kid who only had to worry about picking which toy he wanted to play with next.

My insides were burning. And then it happened again, not too long after the first time.

My dad would often let other kids around the neighborhood come along on our family trips, so they could have different experiences and see more of the world than you could in the heart of Fort Lauderdale. Pop liked to give as many kids as he could a great time, so, when we did go on one of these trips, he let us all pick a friend to take with us. Well, unfortunately, my brother, Leroy, chose his buddy who had violated my friend and me. Leroy didn't know any better—this guy was one of his best friends and Leroy had no idea what he was up to.

We stayed overnight in a motel and all of us were sleeping in the same room. You'd think that would give me a degree of safety—at least I did. But, unbelievably, the guy tried to get me to do it again with him. There was a whole bunch of people asleep right close to us and here he was, coming on to me.

I wasn't having it. At first, I tried to ignore it and pretended like I was asleep too. He wouldn't stop, so I finally had to threaten to say something to the others about what he was doing.

That stopped him. And he never tried it again.

That didn't make me feel any more powerful or better about the situation, but at least I had shut him down. I still felt bad when my brother brought him over to the house to hang, but, again, Leroy didn't know anything about it—why wouldn't he bring his friend over?

A couple of years later, the guy became a crackhead and he and my brother finally went their separate ways. To be honest, he had had kind of a tragic life. He had lost his mom and dad and was living with his brother when all this happened. Still, it was hard to sympathize. When I went down to the elementary school to play ball, I would see him and wonder who else he might have victimized.

The knife I now took everywhere with me was only a small visible sign of the effect his actions had on me. Inside, the impact was much bigger. My life was never the same after that incident. Time seemed to start moving faster and I started acting tougher. But it wasn't just me that was changing. A lot of externals were also changing, and not for the better.

The upshot was that, way before I was ready for it, my childhood was definitely over.

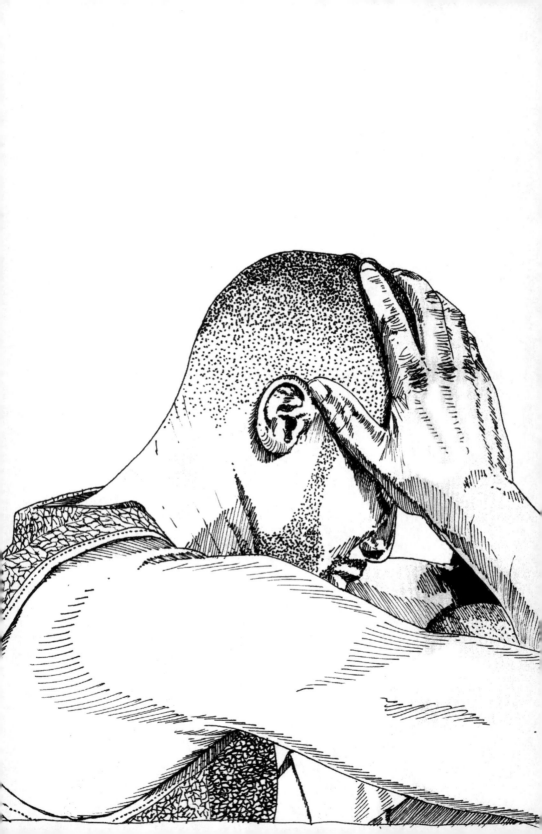

THE BREAKDOWN:
PART TWO

L.A.

SUDDENLY, I WASN'T HUNGRY.

I lost my appetite and I didn't want to eat. After what happened in Seattle with that guy in the restroom, I just didn't feel right. I still felt like something was after me. And I began to feel like time was running out.

But there was another charity event in Los Angeles I had to appear at next. I couldn't let the sponsors or my friends down. I had to keep going, even though I felt I was suddenly operating at a different frequency. It seemed like the world had changed around me—even though it was just me that was transforming.

I made it to the event—and the funny thing was, I gave one of my best speeches at one of these charity events— *ever*. I hit the zone. Suddenly, when I was talking, I found the passion within me that I had when I slam-dunked on somebody or hit a three-pointer. I felt the same incredible satisfaction I experienced on the court when I reached out to the people in that room and spoke my truth. I *connected*.

35

Afterward, I saw for myself that I was right in feeling that way. Everybody from five-year-olds to fifty-year-olds came up to me after the event was over, approaching me with tears in their eyes, giving me hugs. They told me how inspiring my words of encouragement were and how much of a difference the food GameTyme had delivered that day was going to make to their families for months to come. Hell, gang-bangers were coming up and giving me hugs, saying things like, "Yeah, homie, we're going to do a better job of protecting and making safe zones." Some guy even told me, "Man, you should be the spokesman for the Salvation Army." All that positive energy coming at me did my spirit good; relief filled my heart because I had accomplished what I had set out to in L.A.

Why did I deliver so well on the heels of that trauma in Seattle? In retrospect, I believe it's because the darkness that had overwhelmed me the night before had also empowered me. I was more determined than ever to deliver on my responsibility to the kids that would be coming to see us, because I owed them the best that I could give. That morning, I pulled myself together and worked out, even though my spirit was low and my emotions were running high. I was feeling very sensitive—even on the verge of crying. And the toughest part of all was that I didn't know why I was feeling these extreme emotions.

So yeah, I was ecstatic that I had overcome all that and delivered. Back in my room after the event, however, that high was gone—and the negative was back with a vengeance to cut me off at the knees.

I can't explain what happened to me in my room that

night. But again, it felt like I was being attacked by something that wasn't of God. I don't want to pretend I really knew what was going on, I'm just trying to describe what it felt like. Whatever "it" was, it was attacking my mind, it was attacking my body and it was attacking my spirit. Everything about me was under siege.

So I called out to the Lord in a way I hadn't since I was a kid in church.

I was raised going to church on Sundays and taught by my mother about Jesus Christ. I felt that spiritual connection as a child. But, as I got older, as I became a teenager and hung out more on the streets, drinking, playing basketball, dealing with girls, and just living life like any kid my age, I lost that connection a little bit—and I gave up the time I used to make for the Lord.

I had tried to regain that connection in my adult life with my charity work, my family, and how I conducted myself in the NBA. I wanted to be closer to the Lord, but I was still holding back 5 percent. I kept 5 percent in my pocket that wasn't right with God and that I wasn't proud of. That 5 percent brought me profound pain, because it involved bad decisions I had made that could hurt people I loved.

That night, when I felt like I was battling for my very soul, I felt like I had to take that 5 percent out of my pocket, give it up, and make sure it never made its way back in again. I wanted to return home a changed man, a man who was at peace with God and with his life. I wanted the anxiety, the fear, and the anger to be *gone*.

But the darkness wasn't done with me yet. As a matter of fact, the real battle had just begun.

TURNOVER

THE BOTTLES HIT THE COURT with a loud crash and shattered.

Broken glass flew everywhere, covering the asphalt. Nobody was going to be playing ball there for awhile.

My friend and I were the ones who had thrown the bottles, the same friend I was molested with. We were pissed.

This was the court at the elementary school down at the end of the street from my house, close to where the incident happened. We still went down to that court to play, but this time, some bigger kids were playing and they wouldn't let us join in.

So—we decided to get back at them.

Back then, kids would collect empty soda bottles and return them for deposit money to the store houses that sold them. So we got ourselves a couple of empty bottles each and went and smashed them on the court. We didn't get to play? Neither did they. If we were gonna get shut out, everybody was.

I guess you could call it typical stupid kid stuff. But with the two of us, it was a little more. We both had that anger and it was asserting itself. We were growing tougher and more independent. And we weren't about to trust the older kids anymore.

That's because we were becoming older kids ourselves. When you get into adolescence, the simple and childish way you look at things breaks apart. You see more and more of how the world really works. You question things. You notice what's wrong.

You act out.

In my case, that process was accelerated by not only what had happened to me—but what was happening around me, both in my home and my community. And that resulted in my participating in some less-than-admirable activities, just because of my building anger.

Let's start with the community. My neighborhood was changing. Drugs had always been around, but a new and much more powerful player was suddenly in the mix—crack. Crack cocaine was getting a hard grip on the area. It first showed up a few years after I was born, and because it was such a huge high for such a low price, it spread like wildfire in most poverty-stricken areas in the mid to late 80s.

Unfortunately, it is a very extreme drug—you hit it one time, you are hooked. I saw a lot of people get addicted, even in our own family, although I was fortunate enough to see a lot of people recover from it as well. But I saw too many of the former and not enough of the latter. That's why when, every so often, somebody asks me if I ever tried crack, my answer is quick, loud, and only two words:

WHAT'S DRIVING YOU???

HELL NO.

I saw way too much damage from that stuff growing up. I mean, all you had to do was look at a crackhead to know you shouldn't do it. Most kids my age stayed away from the drug at the get-go, because they saw what happened to the older kids who did it. Whitney Houston said it best—"Crack is whack." We were also lucky enough to be educated about it through the Drug Abuse Resistance Education (D.A.R.E.) program in our school, a nationwide effort that began in the mid 80s as a response to the increase in drug usage. The D.A.R.E. instructors focused on crack in their lesson plans, because it had become a big problem—and I mean, a really big problem. It was a *really,* really big problem.

So, yeah, my age group was by and large too scared to do crack—but some weren't too scared to profit from it. They became dealers. In a place where it was hard to make one dollar, there were a lot of guys in my grade coming to school with hundreds of them in their pockets.

Unfortunately, all that did was make crack more available to ruin more lives; you didn't have to look far to find examples all over the neighborhood. I saw mothers of my friends, mothers I used to know and love, selling their bodies on a corner—I would help my friends pull them off the street. No question, families were being broken up by crack.

And crime quickly escalated. It felt like people were breaking into your house or car every other night—and that was suddenly a whole new and extremely stressful part of everyday life that had to be dealt with. There weren't any police in our neighborhood routinely patrolling our

41

streets to protect us from break-ins, so we had to protect ourselves. As the youngest, I wasn't in that position so much, but I saw my dad and my brothers spring into action more than once.

One time, I even saw my mom take care of business. A crackhead busted into our house and wanted to steal our TV for drug money. She actually fought him off with God! I remember her yelling at him, "Uh uh! You drop that TV right now in the name of Jesus! I rebuke that demon that's in you, you get out of my house!" My brother, Leroy, and I went to get sticks to help her fight him off, but we didn't need them—my mom got him out the door with the Lord! Now, if my dad was there, he would have shot him. He was that kind of guy; he would do anything to protect his family.

And once, at a very young age, even I had to take care of business. My mom was a drug counselor for a while when crack usage was skyrocketing, so there were actually times when we would have several recovering crackheads living in our home at one time; we had the room for them because my brothers had left for college. Sometimes these crackheads were close friends or relatives of my mom, but still, they were in bad shape. I remember one woman who was staying with us grabbing a knife and going after my cousin, threatening to kill him. I moved as fast as I could and I grabbed her arm just as she was trying to stab him. Fortunately, I was quick enough to stop what could have been a deadly attack.

Because crack was so prevalent and was hitting so many friends and family members, you didn't know who to trust. There were a lot of functioning crackheads at the time—

meaning they could work a job, carry on an ordinary conversation, and seem like awesome people—but you could never forget they were crackheads. If you did, you'd be a lot poorer for it.

For instance, I might spend the night at a friend's house and that friend might have a crackhead uncle visiting. Well, if you left your wallet laying around in a room, then, boom, that twenty bucks you spent two or three weeks saving up? It would be gone the second you weren't paying attention or went in a different room.

You just never knew who the drug would take control of—and how that person might do you wrong. A good friend of my oldest brother, Eric, became a crackhead. This was someone who was close to our family—my dad had been mentoring him, because he didn't have a dad of his own. Pop helped him pay for his prom and other important life events like that, so his teen years wouldn't be lacking; Pop would do that for a lot of kids in the neighborhood.

Well, in this case, the saying "No good deed goes unpunished" comes to mind. We were all out somewhere and Eric's friend broke into our house, looking to steal stuff he could sell to feed his crack habit. He didn't know we had an alarm installed, and he set it off—so the police came to see what was going down. Was he busted? Not by a long shot. He went ahead and told the cops, "Oh, I'm sorry, y'all. This is my uncle's house. This is just a misunderstanding." And, because he could identify us all by our names, the police believed him and left.

When we came home, he was still in the house—grabbing everything he thought he could sell for some good money. We chased him, but he got away carrying out whatever he could hold. Nothing we could do about it. Make no mistake, crackheads run fast. You ain't catching no crackhead.

While crack took its toll outside the walls of our home, a downturn in our family's financial situation took its toll on the inside. Starting when I was in sixth grade, we weren't so comfortable—because Pop's business suddenly wasn't making as much money.

I'm not sure what happened. As I mentioned earlier, my dad had a very profitable partnership with a local funeral home and even located his shop next to it. Well, one day that was over. I saw my dad get into a fight with the manager of the funeral home—and when I say "fight," I'm talking about fists and everything. Pop won—he ended up really whaling on him—but the business lost and he ended up relocating the flower shop, because that partnership was gone. At the same time, there was a lot more competition out there; dad no longer had the market on flowers in the community all to himself.

With that downturn in the business came a reckoning with a couple of my father's other bad habits. He liked to gamble and he was overly generous with other people in the community. I've already detailed how he helped out a lot of kids; he enjoyed being that guy. For another example, he would take busloads of neighborhood kids to skating rinks—and I also remember him actively passing out condoms from his business when AIDS began to be a problem. He would even hire crackheads to clean our floors. He wanted the community to thrive despite its poverty, but that was a heavy load for anybody to lift, especially somebody whose business suddenly wasn't doing as well. He was way too giving, helping people a lot more than they would ever want to, or could, help him.

But, because we were considered to be one of the more affluent families in the community (we all went to college, we owned our own businesses, owned our own home), people looked to us when they needed a hand. My dad was seen as a positive example of how to earn a living and give back to the community. And he was loved as a person—he was a great entertainer and just really, really fun to be around. He had the gift of gab as well as an incredible, disarming spirit. He could quickly make strangers feel comfortable, safe, and protected.

But, like every other person on this planet, he was not perfect. I inherited some of those flaws, as well as many of his great qualities. But, for the most part, my Pop was… well, he was my buddy, plain and simple. From an early age, I got a lot of awesome business training thanks to him. I was exposed to other affluent black businessmen, and I was even sent out to talk to churches that Pop had flower contracts with in order to keep the relationship in good shape. It felt like every day he gave me some kind of mission to accomplish, whether it was for his business or my basketball. He would call me "Bubba" when he gave me these things to do, as in "Hey, Bubba, you've got to run these deliveries for me," or "Hey, Bubba, get back to the store and pick up those flowers."

I remember one time I didn't have my driver's license yet, and all my older siblings were away. Well, my dad had a wedding to do and he needed my help. Suddenly, I was driving a delivery from Fort Lauderdale to Pompano Beach, about ten miles away—with no license! But that was part of working with Pop. I had to learn to be resourceful at a very early age, just like he did. I had to make sacrifices for the family, and my father trusted me enough to do things I maybe wasn't ready do. He thought I was ready—he would just say, "Bubba can do it." He and my mom always taught us everything we needed to know along the way, without sugarcoating anything. They gave me the tools to be a man.

Still, my dad didn't get all the education or outside experience he needed to keep the business as strong as possible. Don't get me wrong—I am proud as a son could be of what my father accomplished, because he did amazing things with his life despite everything that was against him. Still, because he lived in the same area code his whole life (until I was able to buy him and my mom a condo of their own after my NBA success), he, through no fault of his own, had a limited perspective on what you could and should do with a business.

That meant the floral business survived, but at a lower level, because Pop only knew so much. He put more into us than he had put into himself, and my wife and I are doing the same with our kids: we're putting more into them. Their education is better, their study habits are better, and their world is bigger because they're more traveled than we are. From my father's limited perspective, he did as well as he could with the situation.

As I entered sixth grade, things had changed and I could sense a lot of hard years were ahead of me. My older siblings went off to college and financially things at home went down. We went from one extreme—living very, very comfortably and very, very well—to another. I remember there were a few years when I was a teenager where we didn't have a phone in the house, because suddenly we couldn't afford one. And at that age, especially before cell phones, the home phone was everything.

So yeah, when I threw those bottles on the basketball court, when I smashed that glass all around to keep the older kids off, it wasn't just about basketball. It was about everything. I was making a statement.

And that was leading to a wild and dangerous year where I would have to decide just what kind of man I wanted to be.

TRANSITION OFFENSE

SIXTH GRADE. That's when you went to middle school in my neighborhood. I was out of the performing arts elementary school and into Rogers Middle School (it's not called that anymore, it's now an alternative school). I was in a whole different environment and a whole different place.

It was the year I was at my worst. I was acting out in class, not turning in assignments, talking back to teachers, and skipping school. I did it all and I did it all too much. I was keeping different company too—with older guys from a different neighborhood. I started smoking and I started drinking. After school— or even during school!—we'd buy a cigarette for ten cents and a wine cooler for ninety-nine cents at a nearby store house.

And I wasn't just smoking cigarettes.

The first time I smoked weed was that year. It was no big deal—it just happened because of who I was hanging out with. We were at a house party when some of the kids started rolling up. Why wasn't it a big deal? Well, I had seen

49

a lot of things in the neighborhood up until that time and was exposed to a lot of stuff that most kids my age weren't. I already talked about seeing what crack was doing to people, and weed seemed like nothing next to that. Truth to tell, it wasn't even considered a real drug by anybody.

I had already started drinking a little a couple of years earlier. Because we had a big-screen TV at our house, my dad would throw parties whenever there was a big boxing match on. Since it was a time before there were a lot of big-screen TVs, a lot of people would come over. That gave Pop the opportunity to do his thing, which was to make sure as many people had as good a time as possible.

At one of those parties, I made my move. I sneaked a beer and went in the bathroom to try it out. Well, I spit that beer out as soon as it hit my taste buds—I thought it was *nasty!*

The next day, I really felt like I wanted to try something stronger. This wasn't that long after I was molested and I was still dealing with a lot, a lot I didn't even understand or know how to explain. So when I got home, and nobody else was there, I fixed myself a real drink. Whatever hard alcohol I used, I mixed it with some Coke, just like I'd seen the adults do. Then I put some ice in it and I took a drink. It was just a small cup, and, yeah, it tasted better than that beer, but it burned inside my chest. I didn't get drunk—I just wanted that taste. And from then on, from time to time, I would have myself a taste.

So yeah, sixth grade was when drinking and smoking were regularly in the mix. Some of our fun was inno-cent; we'd go on what we called "The Adventure." The

WHAT'S DRIVING YOU???

Adventure took place back down by the river that was right in back of my family's house. The river continued down under I-95—we'd follow it and encounter different kinds of fish, crab, birds, raccoons, and even manatees, which were around there a lot at the time. We'd also just talk, smoke, and drink down there too, just chill, you know?

But the fun wasn't always so innocent. Like I said, I was hanging out with older kids, and these older kids would occasionally steal cars. I was in one with some guys when the police got behind us. Was I scared? Oh yeah. The cops didn't pull us over—but I never rode in a stolen car again after that happened.

To tell you the truth, few things in my neighborhood frightened me as much as the cops. The drug dealers in the neighborhood actually looked out for me, believe it or not. They saw to it I didn't get into too much trouble. People knew about my basketball and football skills and they also knew and respected my family, so I was somebody that was looked after even when I didn't know it. There was almost always somebody around that had my back.

I didn't have that feeling with the police. Every encounter I remember having with the cops when I was growing up was about them pulling us over and treating us badly—like we had already done something wrong. As a matter of fact, pretty much everybody in our neighborhood was treated badly by the cops. Yeah, there were always good cops as well as bad cops, but, because the neighborhood had gotten so crime-ridden due to the crack, to them everybody was immediately a suspect. I have to say, since that time, they cleaned up the system and they do a great job now back in my old stomping grounds. But back then, it was too much like the Wild, Wild West.

And just like the Wild, Wild West, there was the occasional gunfire.

It was in sixth grade that I saw my first gun battle. We were at a house party in the Lincoln Apartments, just dancing and having fun. It was about midnight when we saw one cat running outside, and—boom!—we saw shots fired. A guy was running for his life, gun in hand, and somebody else was chasing him with a gun in *his* hand. We all ducked and watched the whole thing go down. Nothing happened, but that was the end of the party—we all ran home after that, because we didn't know what else might happen. Through the years, I found out about plenty of people that got shot in my neighborhood, but nobody close to me ever got murdered when I was young. Lucky for me and even luckier for them.

I might've avoided the bullets, but I couldn't and didn't avoid the fists. Even though there wasn't a gang culture in Fort Lauderdale, you would still end up having to fight kids from other neighborhoods. No shooting, but plenty of beefs and plenty of altercations. You used to have to fight for your neighborhood, especially if somebody would come over into your area.

Sometimes it was a matter of who won a game. We would play our park versus another neighborhood's park in basketball or football—and whoever lost had to fight. It was still kind of innocent, but, at the same time, it toughened me up for life and also for the game. Survival of the fittest—it was cool with me, I didn't have a problem with the concept.

Good thing, because those drug dealers and other guys in the neighborhood, the ones I said were looking out for me? Well, they definitely believed in that survival of the fittest idea—and they wanted to make sure I was as tough as possible for what lay ahead of me. That meant more challenges and more fights.

And there was still one more issue that brought conflict to my doorstep. You might call it class warfare. Because people in the neighborhood thought we were more well-off than we really were, I was considered by some to be "too good for the hood"—and, to those people, that meant I had to be cut down to size.

I took boxing and learned how to fight, so I handled myself okay most of the time. But, that same year, when I was in sixth grade, that's when I remember losing my first fight. There was this older kid who just didn't like me. I don't know why, I don't know what he thought, he just plain did not like me. And one day, after school, when the bus dropped us off, a fight broke out.

But it wasn't a fight between me and this older kid. No, a friend of mine was fighting somebody else—and naturally, I was cheering my buddy on. Well, this older kid didn't seem to think I should be doing that, so he came up to me and said, "Okay, what do *you* want to do?" Suddenly, even though he was bigger and older than me, I was in a position where I didn't think I could back down. I came back with a "What do you want to do?" I didn't want people to think I was scared of this guy.

So we fought. It was quick and I could see I was going to get it bad from him. I didn't want to make that mistake and I stopped the fight. And I learned, from then on, to be smarter about picking my battles. There was no point in taking on someone you knew could easily take you because he was so much older and stronger.

I learned a lot about people that year. You had to, in order to survive. You had to learn at an early age about how to deal with bullies, not to mention drug-dealing classmates who made more money than the teachers. I found I had good people skills—I could talk to those guys just as well as I could talk to the people at the churches I went to on behalf of my dad's business. You had to know how to talk to everyone at every different level. The secret, I believed, was to treat everyone with respect. When you give respect, generally you get it back.

That same year, I was suddenly earning a lot of respect in sports. I had a breakout year in football—I played for a local youth team, the Western Tigers, where I scored almost twenty touchdowns as the running back.

And, when it came to basketball, I was proving my worth in more ways than one. This was the year when my dad started taking me to different courts to play people. One-on-one, two-on-two, we'd play other people in other places. Sometimes it was just to build up my reputation—and sometimes it was for cold hard cash. Maybe it would be for two dollars, maybe it would be for five dollars, maybe, if we were really feeling good about our chances, twenty-five or fifty dollars. I even had drug dealers betting on me because they knew how good I was getting.

The first time I remember my dad pitting me against somebody else was when, going around the neighborhood, he started noticing a big guy playing on a local court. He thought I could take him and he told the guy that he wanted him to play me. And he told him that, even though I was younger and smaller, I could win out over him. Naturally, that stoked this guy's competitive fires.

So, on a day when Pop and I were driving around together, he happened to spot the big guy in the park. He pulled over and jumped out, yelling, "I got my boy with me!" And he turns to me and says, "Go play him, chief."

Now I'm about five feet, six inches tall at this time. I take a look at this guy, who's six feet, three inches and almost three years older than me, and I think that this is a real *bad* idea. And I'm like, "Dad, Pop, you can't be serious, dawg."

But dad wasn't kidding. He was like, "Boy, you better go out there and play him. I've been talking you up. You better go out there and play him. Bubba, go *kick his ass*. You can do it, Bubba. Go kick his ass."

Whoa.

Well, as you know, when my Pop gave me a mission, I did my best to accomplish it. So I went and gave it my all—and damn if I didn't beat him real quick! My dad couldn't have been happier. He gave me about ten bucks and took me out to dinner, telling me, "Hey, I don't care who you play, how big they are, or how nasty they play. You can beat anybody!" Then he went out to brag to all his friends about what happened.

That may have been the first time I realized just *how* good at bball I was.

Yeah, that year, I was growing up fast. Too fast. Like I said, I was hanging out with an older, tougher group and they were up to a lot of no good. That brought me to a real turning point.

One day, my group decided the goal was going to be to go around and knock a few people out. Bums—we'd just whomp on 'em and knock 'em down. Actually, as I write these words, this unsavory activity has suddenly been reported in the media and labelled "The Knockout Game," and treated as though it were something that just started happening in 2013. Well, considering this was around when I was only in sixth grade, it's far from a new phenomenon.

And, by the way, to those who would ask, "How could anybody do this kind of thing?", the deeper question to me is "What's the root cause of this kind of out-of-nowhere anger? How do we stop the vicious cycle of violence that comes out of poverty?" I don't have the answers, but I do know it's an issue that we need to deal with. I do what I can to this day to try and inspire young kids to abandon this kind of behavior—but there is no doubt that it's hard to grow past the environment they're born into.

Anyway, I went along with the plan, but when one of the group suddenly said, "Hey, we got one," I suddenly knew I didn't want to be a part of this. I knew it was the absolute wrong path for me. I personally didn't do anything to anyone, but there was no way to feel good about being involved in that kind of situation. I felt just as guilty as the guy who had thrown the punches—and I didn't want to end up *being* that guy the next time around.

So, I broke away—and a few of my closest buddies followed me and went back to a place where we would hang.

WHAT'S DRIVING YOU???

And we decided we weren't going to be a part of that kind of action any longer.

People believed in me and my basketball skills. Thanks to my Pop, I had seen just for myself how good I was. I knew I didn't want to throw away what potential I had. If I had a chance to get a basketball scholarship, if I had even a microscopic chance to make it to the NBA, I needed to focus and I needed to keep out of trouble.

And that's just what I was going to do.

TIME-OUT

YEAH, I GREW UP in what could be a pretty rough neighborhood and learned how to deal with that environment. So I know firsthand the challenges kids can face in that kind of neighborhood—which is why I make a point of reaching out to them through the charity I work I do. That's why I want to take a quick "time-out" to share the advice I give them to anybody reading this book who is currently in the position I was in growing up.

First of all, it's easy to fall in with the wrong crowd, as I did briefly. Too easy, as a matter of fact. When you're with the wrong people, you start getting into the wrong things, as I just told you about. Me, when I saw where that particular road would take me, I made a U-turn—*immediately.* You can't ease out of that kind of situation—you have to make the break quick and clean. Once you do that, surround yourself with positive people as much as possible, people you can learn from, who will motivate and inspire you, and lead you to a better life.

If your home situation is difficult or if your neighborhood is too harsh, try and find a safe haven where you feel okay to do your homework, or just to play and hang out. Whether it's a Boys and Girls Club or an after-school program, find that safe haven—I consider that to be very important. If you're always looking over your shoulder, that wears you down.

Finally, look for the right adult mentor (hopefully, that mentor can be a parent) and discuss what's going on and what's challenging you in your life. Ask for advice; don't think you have to deal with everything all by yourself. You're not alone. So find that person you can go and get that guidance from. And by the way, you can have more than one mentor—I certainly did.

Remember, you can always rise above your surroundings if you seek out the people and the places that can nourish your spirit, your mind, and your body. Respect those around you and respect your neighborhood.

But above all, always respect yourself.

THE BREAKDOWN: PART THREE

BACK HOME

I CAME HOME FROM THE SEATTLE-L.A. charity trip feeling exhausted and dehydrated. I wasn't eating, I wasn't sleeping, and I was still grappling with the dark visions that kept invading my head.

I was beginning to display all the symptoms of Post Traumatic Stress Disorder (PTSD), even though I had never spent one day in combat. Suddenly, I felt like I was under a continual low shot clock.

As most of you know, when you're playing a basketball game and you have the ball, you have a limited time to shoot for a basket or pass it to a teammate so he can make the shot. You're at the mercy of the shot clock—and when it's down to the last few seconds and you hear the final countdown, "3...2...1...", you know you have to make your move *now*. That's a pressure-packed situation, especially when you're the one controlling the ball.

Well, that's how I started to feel ALL the time back home—and that's when people really thought I was losing my mind. Every decision, every task, every phone call, everything I needed to do felt like life or death, even if whatever was involved wasn't all that important.

Everything was crucial to me. The shot clock was always about to run out, at least in my head.

I continued to repent for my sins, because I felt like I was literally about to die with all these negative emotions and visions hanging on to me. Yeah, I thought death was actually chasing me. At this point, I completely gave myself over to the Lord. I told the Holy Spirit that I would be totally led by Him from this point on and not be a slave to my past.

Again, I thought this was purely a religious thing, that I had done wrong and I was being punished for it. While I give full credit to God for getting me through this ordeal, the fact was that I had PTSD—but I had no idea I had it and had no idea what it did to you. I thought, like many of you reading this probably think, that it was something that only affected men and women in the military who had been through stressful combat situations.

It had only been about two weeks since my problems started to manifest, and they just kept getting worse. Again, my appetite was completely gone.

My family, of course, noticed the change in me. The kids were like, "Something's wrong with daddy." And yeah, there most certainly was. Something so wrong that I couldn't take it anymore. The thought of ANY more pressure coming down on me was unbearable—and that's why I finally said to my wife words that would have been unthinkable coming out of my mouth two weeks earlier.

"I don't think I can play anymore."

WHAT'S DRIVING YOU???

I felt so damaged and drained, I felt so much stress, that I knew I was in no shape to get back on the court with the Celtics. But I wanted to talk it over with other people in my life. I started talking to other friends and family members, telling them that I wanted to retire from my NBA career.

I was, of course, met with disbelief from all sides—after all, I had a solid $1.4 million contract with one of the great basketball teams in America. We had gone to Game 7 of the Eastern Conference Finals last season. I was going to give up the dream just like that? The money, the celebrity, and everything that came with being a pro basketball player—I was going to throw all that out the window?

More importantly, I was going to give up the thing I loved to do more than anything else in the world? The thing I had been doing since the day I could first play with a ball as a child?

When I told people I wanted to quit, the number one question they asked was, "What's going on with you?" That would have been my response if the shoe was on the other foot.

But I didn't have an answer for them. I didn't know what was going on with me. I just knew my mental shot clock was running out—and I couldn't take it anymore.

RUN AND GUN

WHEN I WAS AROUND TEN, my mom took me to see a pastor who was visiting our church. Now, this pastor was known to us as a prophet. This was nothing unusual to encounter in our neighborhood, where God and spirituality were considered to be potent and active forces in all our everyday lives. I had seen everything from healings to exorcisms growing up, so a pastor who was also deemed a prophet was nothing out of the ordinary.

However, that night, he saw me as something out of the ordinary, even though my age had just reached double digits. He singled me out and asked me to come forward.

He brought me up in front of everybody and said I would be going to the NBA in the future. Not only that, but I was going to achieve more than I ever thought possible, even beyond playing in the pros, and be an important example to a lot of people.

This was a big deal to everyone in the room, except for one person—me. Now, you'd think any ten-year-old kid would want to hear those kinds of words—but I guess I *was* different, because I already felt all that inside me! I certainly don't want to sound arrogant or egotistical, but I have to be honest; what the pastor said about me was *something I already knew about myself.*

Yeah, maybe I was just a crazy, deluded little kid, but the truth was I knew how good I was becoming. And I knew I wasn't going to stop until I got to the NBA—nor would I let anyone stop me. There were a few occasions where I had more faith in my own abilities than some pivotal people around me.

Some of that faith came from years of competing at a high level. Besides my neighborhood one-on-one encounters, where my dad and even local drug dealers would bet on me winning out over seemingly bigger and stronger opponents on the court, I had also been playing on an incredibly successful travel team since I was six.

For those of you unfamiliar with travel teams, basically what happens is the best young players from an area get organized into a team by someone, usually the parent of one of the players. The travel team then does just what its name implies—it travels to other areas, usually in the same state, to play other travel teams made up of the best kids in that community. This usually happens during the summer when there's no school, so there's time to train and make the trips.

For a young player who shows promise, the travel-team experience at an early age can be essential to developing as an athlete. By playing against the best at a young age, you learn what it takes to really compete at the highest level (well, the highest level for six- to fourteen-year-olds!) and you start thinking about how to build your skills to meet that elite standard. And the really cool thing is that you also get a realistic idea of how good you are *outside* your own neighborhood.

The parent who ran our travel team, the Florida Road-runners, all those years was Judge Zebedee Wright, who happened to be the first black judge appointed in Broward County, where we lived. The judge was a great man I learned a lot from—he mentored lots of kids like me. Me and a lot of other kids thought of him as a great father to have when you were away from your own father. More importantly, he acted as the *only* father to a lot of boys who didn't have one of their own at home.

Judge Wright loved coaching the travel team so much that, even when his son decided to stop playing, he continued putting our travel team together—and of course, my dad was on hand to help out and add his support, as he was at every stage of my career until he passed. Pop even helped sponsor a few kids on the team, as every boy had to help pay for the team's expenses.

One big reason the judge kept coaching us was...well, we always won! Every year, we were the top team, because we had a *lot* of talent on board. Two of the guys I played with, besides me, made it to the pros—one of them played basketball internationally and another played in the NFL. Several others in the travel team program also went on to the NFL.

In any event, we beat all the other travel teams in the league and took the championship every year, every time.

That kind of repeat performance can't help but build your confidence along with your skills—which is exactly what happened with me. I knew I was good—heck, my own father was betting his own money on me at a time when his bankroll was starting to shrink.

So, yeah, when that pastor predicted my future, I felt its truth. I wanted a career in basketball more than anything else—I felt it was the pathway to a better life for my entire family, not just me, and more importantly, I loved the game. I went to sleep watching NBA compilation videos of people like Michael Jordan and dreamt about when I would be playing alongside legendary players like him.

That's why the kind of stuff I was pulling in sixth grade stopped dead cold when I started seventh.

Reaching seventh grade was significant for one simple reason—I could finally play on the middle school basketball team. And to play on that team, I had to keep my grades at a certain level and not get in trouble.

My future was on the line and the past had to be respected. My brothers had played on that middle school team and so had my sister—they had all made their individual marks. It was my turn and I wanted to make a name for myself, as well as help the school keep its winning ways. And I knew I could, because I wasn't the only good player there; we had some of the best basketball players who would ever play for the school all together at the same time on the same team, including a few guys from our awesome travel teams.

This was my time; this was *our* time and I intended to focus completely on achieving all I could. Don't get me wrong, I still had my weekend fun—I would hang out with my friends and drink and dance and smoke, that was just the culture around the neighborhood. But I wasn't going to be self-destructive. I wasn't going to jeopardize my future with foolish actions. If anything, I would be the opposite— and build toward that NBA dream I was determined to live for real.

But that dream wasn't the only thing fueling my motivation. There was something else in the mix that fueled my competitiveness and my edge. That something else was how the molestation that had happened to me years earlier had affected my personality.

To put it bluntly, I was never as easygoing as I had been before that incident. Suddenly, whatever I was up to with somebody else, I felt I had to be the best— the person who would always one-up the other. Obviously, if we were playing basketball, I wanted to be the one to outplay you. Even if we were just joking back and forth, I wanted to be the one who had the last laugh. I would turn a lot of activities into a competition, a competition that I was always trying to win.

I don't know if that edge came from increased strength or buried anger. Whatever the cause, for the time being, I was able to almost completely channel it into sports. In football (which I still played at that time), I would hit the opposing team as hard as I could. And in basketball, I went for a lot more shots from my position than I really should have. I had become almost fearless.

This all sounds crazy, I know, but everything you encounter in life molds you in some way. We all face different challenges in life, and those challenges shape us and transform us. Sometimes they break us down and destroy us;

71

sometimes they turn what was an ugly duckling into a beautiful swan. For me, at that time, it was definitely the latter. I felt more powerful and confident in my abilities as I grew older. Sometimes overcoming negative events can bring out the champion in you and help you find that spark deep inside. This was the case for me at the time.

The key words in that previous sentence are, "at the time." The other darker half was waiting, biding its time.

In seventh and eighth grade, however, I was on my game on the football field, the basketball court, and academically. I got very good grades without having to work very hard for them outside of school hours; it was that easy for me. *Too* easy for me, as would become evident very soon. On the court, our middle school team lost only *one* game during the two seasons I played for them. Our games would all sell out—*everybody* would come to see them. We were just thirteen and fourteen years old, and we were playing to sell-out crowds!

Near the end of middle school, I realized I wanted to leverage what I had achieved with my team to make what I believed would be the next big step toward achieving my athletic ambitions. Unfortunately, that step would spark a large controversy that would briefly pit my community against my family—as well as drop me into a situation that was difficult from almost every angle.

AWAY GAME

MOST PEOPLE THINK SPORTS SCHOLARSHIPS are only available when you're applying to colleges and universities. What you might not know is that there are also sports scholarships to certain private high schools that want to add talent to their teams.

In my area, there were two private Catholic high schools that provided those kinds of scholarships—St. Thomas Aquinas and Cardinal Gibbons. Now, for a non-Catholic student such as myself, just the basic tuition with expenses could reach up to $10,000 per year. That meant a basketball scholarship for the duration of high school would be worth around $40K.

I wanted one of those scholarships, because I saw it as key to my career and my development. The number one reason for that was, if I went to Dillard, my neighborhood high school (where, as you might recall, I had played basketball as a five-year-old), I wasn't going to be able to play varsity. They told me they didn't think I was ready—but I knew I was. I wanted to prove I was good enough to play with the same juniors and seniors I'd been beating on the local courts since I was a little kid.

And no one was gonna stop me from trying.

What it came down to is, I didn't want the school to judge me without giving me a chance. That kind of rebelliousness was a pattern with me. I never allowed any institution or person to render a final verdict on how good I was. I never had a problem with having to prove myself—I just asked for the opportunity. I thought that was fair.

The number two reason for considering the private school option was that I had seen a couple of other guys in the hood do it. Not only did they get a superior education, but they also became star athletes. They were my role models.

Finally, I wanted to make sure I *did* get the opportunity to go to college.

You have to understand, there was a crazy amount of sports talent in my neighborhood—that's why our middle school team was so good. It was a result of everybody playing so much and so hard in and out of school; football and basketball were a great outlet for energy in the hood. Unfortunately, because most kids did not go on past high school, they didn't get the exposure or the shot at a sports career that might have been possible. Cardinal Gibbons was a pathway to higher education for me.

A few of the best of my middle school teammates were interested in exploring the private school option with me—so we went to talk to St. Thomas, because they were known as having the better basketball program of the two private schools. Unfortunately, they told us they would only take us if all of us would come—and my friends ultimately decided they wanted to stay in the neighborhood and play at Dillard.

That left me on my own to approach Cardinal Gibbons—but my reception there was a lot warmer; they offered me a full scholarship all by my lonesome. Good news, yeah—but also the beginning of a lot of big problems.

Dillard High School was and is a pillar of my childhood community; it shared the same name as the very first black school that was established in the area (which is now the site of a museum). My father went there, most of my relatives in the neighborhood went there, and my brothers and sister went there. Most people didn't go on to college; their last school stop was Dillard. I, of course, had my own long history with the school; I had been going to games there since I was a little kid to watch my brothers play ball and play some myself with a recreational team.

That's why for me to *not* go to Dillard was seen as a betrayal in a lot of people's eyes.

My father took the most heat. Pop had always been a big Dillard booster and had mentored a lot of kids there. He always tried to be there when they needed him. Now, suddenly, he was being called names like "Uncle Tom" and being accused of selling out—not because of anything *he* had done, but because I had chosen to go out of the neighborhood to a primarily white high school.

My folks were both hurt by all the neighborhood opposition to my plans—especially since it was coming from so many people that they had always loved and helped out when they could. Despite the backlash, my parents backed my decision and respected it.

I was lucky to have parents like them; they never pressured me to change my mind. When it came to the major decisions in my life, they would always let me make the call when I was old enough to properly do so. Their attitude was, "Hey, this is your life, we're just here to guide you." When my siblings and I faced crossroads in our lives, they would present us with our options, have us do the research and make the decisions with their input.

Unfortunately, even though it was me who chose Cardinal Gibbons, we all had to weather the storm of neighborhood disapproval together—and we did.

That was problem number one that came out of my decision to go to Cardinal Gibbons. Problem number two came when I actually showed up there on my first day, totally unprepared for the culture shock coming my way.

As I've written, I grew up in a very black neighborhood that was initially created by segregation. Most of us didn't get out much beyond that neighborhood—we really had no "normal" day-to-day social interaction with white people, because there just weren't any around. I almost exclusively encountered white folks only as authority figures. When I worked for my Pop, for example, I would sometimes meet some white businessmen. Other than that, I only interacted with them in adult roles such as teachers, school administrators, and police officers. There was nobody I could just say, "Hey, how are you doing?" to as casually as I could to the people in my neighborhood.

I was in for the exact opposite experience at my new

school. I was suddenly as alone as the typical Gibbons' kid would be in my neighborhood.

Nothing symbolized my cultural journey like that first ride to school. Because the school was a half-hour ride away, my Pop (and later, my brother or a friend) had to drive me there. The school was to the east of us, close to the affluent beach area, and I remember watching out the window and seeing the neighborhoods gradually transform—from the projects in my community to the bigger, more luxurious houses near the ocean, houses like the one I am privileged to live in today. To tell the truth, that daily ride became something I looked forward to—it inspired me to attain a higher quality of life and fueled my aspirations.

But when I first entered that school, I found myself surrounded by classmates who not only had a completely different skin color, but a completely different life experience than mine. I was a fish as far out of water as a fish could get.

Fortunately, I knew a few other guys already going there. One of them, Major Parker, was a grade ahead of me and had already gone through what I was going through—choosing to go to Gibbons instead of his neighborhood school. Luckily, he was helpful and mentored me through the experience.

There were a few other scholarship kids like me at the school (about fifteen of us) that I could talk to about how to adjust to this new experience. And that was critical to helping me deal with this new situation.

But socially, there was no question I didn't fit in, especially at first. Take girls for example. Back in the neighborhood, I was used to most girls liking me to the point where

I took it for granted. At Gibbons...total opposite! That's tough on the male ego.

Now, working in my favor was the fact that rap music, and the black culture associated with it, was breaking through into the mainstream. So, gradually, my friends and I were more accepted—especially as my peers came to know me and my personality. I talked a little rougher than them because of my background, but that smoothed out the longer I was there.

The popularity of rap also led to some very awkward interactions, however—because there were suddenly white kids who wanted to *act* like they were black. One in particular wore his pants low like the rappers and listened to rap music exclusively. This one day, one of my white classmates pointed to him and said to me, "That guy is a real wigga." So I asked, "What does that mean?" He replied, "He's a white..." And *then* he realized what word he would have to say to me next. He kind of stuttered a little and finally said, "...you know."

Yeah, I did know.

And I'm sure a few people said that word to describe me and my friends behind our backs from time to time. Some people did treat me well, but others didn't— and I had to deal with that negative element every school day.

There were some who would only talk to me in a loud, sarcastic black voice, saying things like, "Dawg, wassup dawg? I'm your dawg, wassup brotha?" There were others who still thought the Civil War hadn't been settled and would have Confederate flags on their stuff—they were the scariest. They would stare at me with eyes that said loud and

WHAT'S DRIVING YOU???

clear, "Don't f— with me, I'm not one to f— with."

It was relentless and difficult. I had to learn how to navigate in spite of those backward attitudes—but on some level, they can't help but affect you.

I did have some great positives to fall back on. Remember the travel team I talked about playing on from the time I was six years old—the one that never lost?   Well, here's the funny thing—some of my new basketball teammates at Cardinal Gibbons were guys I had played against since I was six! And despite the fact that our team always kicked their butts, I had a good friendship going with two of them before I even went to Gibbons—as a matter of fact, they were helpful getting me into the school, because they wanted me to play with them, not against them! Don't get me wrong, they always used to give us a good battle—so it was a lot of fun to be able to play on the same side with them now.

There was an even bigger challenge than my social life at Cardinal Gibbons, and that was my schooling. Private school was a lot more challenging than my neighborhood public schools had been. I could skip studying and homework back in middle and elementary school and easily get away with it. I wasn't mature enough to understand how important education was back then. As you know by now, my mindset was directed to the basketball court, not the schoolroom.

Those days were gone in a flash. At Cardinal Gibbons, the class size was much smaller so you couldn't really escape notice if you weren't participating. And you HAD to do all your assignments—period. Some classes had tests every week. Everything was suddenly harder—and a lot more was expected of me. I remember going to Spanish class one day and just putting my head down on the desk, because I was convinced there was NO way I was ever going to figure out how to conjugate verbs in that language.

Even the little stuff got more complicated. In middle school, I could carry all my paperwork in the same small folder from class to class. We weren't expected to have more supplies than that, because they were an extra expense most families couldn't handle. Suddenly, I had to master the fine art of folders and binders— and keep my literature work separated from my algebra work, my history work and social studies work. And in addition to buying all those supplies, my family had to spring for a scientific calculator. They're still expensive now and they were more expensive then—and that cost was a big deal to my folks.

My first report card was a real shock to the system—because my grade point average stood at a 1.5; in other words, just barely a "C." If I went a tenth of a point under that, I would be taken off the basketball team—which maybe would have ended my scholarship and my shot at a good college.

I knew what the problem was—I had no real academic training. No study habits. No structure. No discipline. None of that was ever a big deal at public school— but now I saw how the other half did it. I saw firsthand how a higher level (i.e. wealthier) group of people had access to a much higher class of education—and how people like me were left at a big disadvantage because of it.

But there were many helping hands to guide me through my struggle. Most of the teachers recognized that I was intelligent—I just needed the right kind of guidance to help me develop good study habits. Two teachers in particular, Ms. Hanke and Ms. Burke, made time to give me the tools I needed to turn things around. For example, Ms. Hanke showed me how to do flash cards, because I was doing poorly on my weekly vocabulary tests. Now I was learning how to use words like "belligerent" and "facetious," words I had heard but had never understood.

Between the two of them, they whipped me into shape. My mom helped tutor me at home since we couldn't afford a formal tutor. And it turned out we didn't need one. I kept moving up the grading scale, from that 1.5 to a 1.8; from a 1.8 to a 2.0,; from a 2.0 to a 2.2; from a 2.2 to a 2.5; and a 2.5 to a 2.8. By the end of my sophomore year, I was making a 3.0 every quarter. I had figured out what I needed to do—and I did it.

I singled out those two teachers, but the fact is that all the teachers were phenomenal at Cardinal Gibbons; they all pushed and challenged me in their own unique way.

There was only one teacher I felt treated me in a genuinely disrespectful way. I wasn't a strong reader early on, and this teacher would make it a point to call on me to read aloud. I would struggle, and the rest of the class would whisper and laugh about my bad performance. Because the class was an elective, I started skipping it. It was the only time I quit on a class there. I got in trouble and had to go to detention, but I didn't care. I rebelled against his treatment of me; I just thought, "I'm not dealing with this dude. This dude's got a problem with me." That was definitely a negative—but it was only one among an overwhelming number of positives at the school.

The last big difference between my new school and the rest of my life experience leading up to that point? Cardinal Gibbons was, as I said, a Catholic school. The way they praised the Lord was different from how we did it at the churches I went to. As part of our school curriculum, we were required to go to Mass and to chapel. I was never taught a great deal of Catholicism, but I was responsible for learning certain prayers and other things I was tested on. I didn't mind that. I was happy to learn the different ways people love Jesus Christ. We all shared in Christ's love—although, as I said, some people at the school didn't seem anxious to share that love with *me*. We all had Him in common, however, so the specifics of the Catholic religion never alienated me in the slightest.

Ironically, the more comfortable I got at my new school, the more uncomfortable I became back in my old neighborhood. The vitriol that was directed at my Pop was now heading straight in my direction. I was the one getting called "Uncle Tom" now, as well as "Cracka-Nigga" and "Switch-Out." On the weekends, when I would want to hang out with my old crowd, they'd suddenly start telling me there wasn't room for me. So, in addition to making all those new friends at school, I also had to make new friends in my *old* neighborhood.

Yeah, ninth grade was a huge year of change for me, one of the biggest. It was also the year I got serious about the woman I'm married to today—and the most special person in my life.

TOSHA

MY FIRST REAL RELATIONSHIP came during my freshman year at Gibbons. But it wasn't with anybody there—it was with somebody back in the old neighborhood.

One of my middle school friends was dating somebody and I happened to go along with them to a dance. His girl-friend had one of her friends with her—and when I saw her, I couldn't stop looking at her eyes and her legs. I thought she was amazing. I said to myself, "Man, that's who I need to be hooked up with." I was too shy to talk to her much that night, but later on, I called her and we began to go out together.

Natosha—or "Tosha," as everybody calls her—was the first woman I ever had serious feelings for. When I was younger, I would see her on her aunt's front porch as I rode by on my bicycle and notice her even then. Of course, that's all I could do was notice her—she didn't have the freedom to move around the neighborhood like I did. As a matter of fact, other than going to school, at that age, she wasn't even allowed off the porch because her family was so overprotective.

But now, we were both older and we both felt the connection. It was different being with her—and I was ready to finally try and have a real relationship with someone, one that went beyond just hanging out and having some fun.

It wasn't easy getting that relationship going, I have to tell you. She went to Dillard. I went to Gibbons. My day was already incredibly full; between trying to master my new stringent academics, working out, and basketball practice, my time was very limited.

To add to that super-scheduled scenario, there was also the little matter of me not having a phone to call her on!

Now, right before I started dating Tosha, when I was starting ninth grade at Gibbons, the phone company had crossed their lines or something—and for some reason, our phone was actually working even though we weren't paying for it. And it might still have been working when I finally hooked up with Tosha, if it hadn't been for some gunfire one night.

I was home alone and I heard some shots from next door. I immediately turned off the lights and got down on the floor. Through our patio door, I could see a guy hiding in our backyard. That wasn't good—I didn't know if he had the gun or someone with a gun was gonna come after him.

But, hey, no problem, right? I can call the police! I called 911 and told them what was going on. They asked me what address I was at, I told them and they kept telling me that the phone number I was calling from wasn't registered to that address. I kept telling them that was where I was, and, finally, when some other people on the block started calling about the shooting, they believed me. Unfortunately, they also said they were going to let the phone company know about the problem with the number.

Next morning? No more phone.

When you're at the beginning of a relationship with a person you care about, you want to talk to that person every single day as often as you can. Well, I was lucky if I was able to talk to Tosha just once a day.

Between practice and the long ride home, it would be late by the time I would get home from Gibbons, like between five o'clock and six o'clock. That's when I made the phone rounds. I would walk over to my buddy's house to see if he was home from his practice so I could use his phone to call Tosha. If he wasn't there, I'd hit my *other* buddy's house and try to use his phone. If he wasn't there, then I would have to walk even farther to my grandma and granddad's house.

That was my half of the equation. On Tosha's side, she had cheerleading practice and she had to take a bus home from there. And when she did get home, her mom might take her somewhere to eat or she might have somewhere else she had to be that particular night. So, by the time I finally got access to somebody's phone, there was a good chance she might not even be on the other end to talk to!

That was what I put myself through every night after coming home from school. I had that one or two hour window to try and catch up with her on the phone and that was all. I had to get back home by a certain time because I had to tackle my homework and get to sleep so I could be ready for everything I had to do the *next* day.

KEYON L. DOOLING

Yeah, I went through all that almost every school day. As you might imagine, you don't do all that unless this is a girl you definitely want in your life. I could feel it big-time— because when the day was over and I hadn't managed to talk to her, it would end up being a long, lonely night for me.

It was very important for me to keep that relationship alive (as it is to this day)— and we managed it right through senior year. Soon, college would put too many miles between us, however—and temporarily disrupt the special bond we shared.

PLAYER CONTROL

SO LET'S MOVE ON to the the *real* reason I went to Cardinal Gibbons—basketball.

Although I had always played football every season in addition to basketball up until this time, that sport had to go because of my new school. Being on a scholarship worth tens of thousands of dollars meant I couldn't risk getting hurt on the gridiron.

It was another crossroads for me. Athletically, it was time to put all I had on the court and nowhere else. As a result, my development in the game during this time was profound.

Much of that was due to Mark Wilson, my new coach at Cardinal Gibbons. He believed in me. He knew how my middle school team had dominated our league and he knew I was an integral part of its success. It's always been important to me (and to any player, really) that I have a coach who has faith in my abilities, and Coach Wilson gave me that kind of support.

However, just as academics at my new high school were more structured and demanding, basketball was suddenly a different game too—in a way that frustrated me and drove my Pop in-*sane*! And suddenly I was wondering if I had made a huge mistake leaving my neighborhood's style of ball at this juncture.

All my life, I had been playing an inner-city game of basketball with other inner-city kids. While there was certainly some structure in place, my previous teams had been happy to ignore it if it brought us another two or three points. In other words, if I had a shot, I took it—or my Pop would let me have it. If I didn't respond to his call to "Shoot it, Bubba!", I would hear about it later.

Basically, the way we played back in the hood was organized chaos. We would run fast and trap, be relentless, and play hard. We weren't out to observe the niceties of the game—we were out to win.

And, like they say, you can't argue with success, right?

Well, Coach Wilson could and would. Now, it was almost all about organization and structure; we were running plays, something I really didn't have much experience with. The discipline of the game suddenly became key and I had to get on board with that discipline. In some ways, it was a welcome adjustment—as I mentioned before, my brothers and I had regularly watched NBA tapes to study the game at that advanced level, and it was fun to be able to now put that knowledge into play.

In other ways, however, that discipline was a problem for both me—and Pop.

My whole life, I had always played point guard. For me,

WHAT'S DRIVING YOU???

I thought it was the most fun position to play because you had the ball most of the time and I like to dribble; when you're dribbling the ball, everyone's looking at you. Guard for me was always the vocal person on the court, the leader. It's often compared to being a quarterback for a football team. Also, to be practical, I always thought I would be kind of small so I figured it was the natural position for me.

Traditionally, however, the point guard is more of a set-up man than a shooter. He's supposed to get the ball to the players who have the best chance at scoring. But up until that point, nobody had really cared if I did the scoring myself or not—what was important was that somebody had scored. That's just how our neighborhood teams played—if you thought you could get it in, you went for it.

And I did, as often as I could.

That's what counted in the hood, how many times you got the ball through the hoop—and I did, a lot of times. At Gibbons, it was a completely different story, because I now had to play the position the way it was supposed to be played; Coach Wilson insisted on it and he was right. As a result, my scoring stats suddenly sank. I only averaged nine points and five assists a game as a freshman, and twelve and six as a sophomore.

Okay numbers for a point guard. HORRIBLE numbers for my dad.

He heard about how my old teammate on the middle school team was now averaging about twenty to twenty-five points a game at Dillard High—everybody in the hood made sure he heard about it! They now had a new excuse to bad-mouth my decision to Pop and make him feel as though I was going to be left behind in the dust at my new school.

So he was after me to shoot more. He wasn't just afraid of the blowback from his friends; he was afraid I wasn't going to shine as a player like I had in the past and that would affect my future prospects. When I was on the court, though, I had to listen to Coach Wilson and not "Coach Leroy." That meant when Pop yelled, "Shoot it, Bubba," I wasn't always going to respond. More often than not, I wouldn't.

That made for some long car rides home after a game.

When I hadn't made as many shots as he thought I should, he would drive quietly and breathe hard, like somebody who couldn't quite get enough air in. He would keep shifting and moving positions in his seat. And even though he wasn't saying a word, he was communicating very clearly, believe you me.

Finally, anxious to get it over with, I would say, "What's up, Pop? Just go ahead and say it."

Then the dam would burst. "Man, Godd—, Godd—, I ain't gonna come to this mother-f—ing game to see you pass that mother-f—ing ball every time! Come on, Bubba! I'm gonna go to the Dillard games from now on, they shoot that thing! I just can't take it anymore!"

Pop would threaten not to—but he always showed up at my games. Always. All throughout my NBA career, I would see him in the stands. He couldn't really be yelling "Shoot it, Bubba" at me at that point, but, when he caught me looking at him, he had this little motion he'd do where he flicked his fingers off his sleeve—that was his silent signal for "Shoot it, Bubba."

WHAT'S DRIVING YOU???

My father's encouragement is the thing I miss the most to this day—even though that encouragement didn't always come out in the nicest way—or with the nicest words attached to it!

But ...

I had to learn the game as it was supposed to be played, especially if I wanted to advance to the pros; I needed to become more professional and polished in my approach. What Coach Wilson taught me ultimately helped me a great deal, even though, at the time, it was incredibly frustrating. As a matter of fact, for awhile, I did think about leaving and going back to Dillard—and to the brand of basketball I had grown up with.

I stuck it out, though, and I'm glad I did. I was a starter on the Gibbons team from the get-go—and, on February 25, 1995, I experienced one of my most thrilling moments on the court ever, when I made a game-winning free throw with 3.4 seconds to spare (and that was two minutes after I hit a three-pointer to put us ahead for the first time in the fourth quarter). That point broke a tie and sent our varsity team to the Florida state high school finals.

The newspaper headline in the Fort Lauderdale newspaper, the *Sun Sentinel,* said it all:

Freshman's Cool Keys Gibbons' Win

That was *me* the paper was talking about. And in the article below that great headline, Major Parker, my mentor on the team, said of me, "Forget calling him a freshman. He's a big-time player."

KEYON L. DOOLING

I was also quoted for one of the first times in my basketball career in that write-up —and I ended up quoting somebody else! The reporter asked me what it felt like when I made the free throws. Well, I had just seen the movie *Above the Rim,* starring one of my favorites, Tupac Shakur, and I borrowed a line of dialogue from the character Duane Martin had played, saying, "I was just thinkin' 'bout spreadin' my fingers and poppin' my wrist."

Unfortunately, we didn't advance in the state tournament, but still, I had to remember that I was a freshman and I was the starting point guard on a state final four team. That was a big deal.

I knew it was going to work out for me at Gibbons as far as the basketball went. I had done well, even though I still wasn't fully grown and I was playing against mostly older, bigger kids. I could hold my own and I was only going to keep getting better.

My teammates had also been awesome to me my first year. Even though the white kids outnumbered the black ones by more than 2-to-1 margin on the team, they showed me that the only thing that was different was our background and our skin color. As far as everything else went, they were just like me. And that was an important thing for me to learn.

As a matter of fact, the further I got out of the hood, the more I found out that everybody was basically the same. I'm proud that I've become as "colorblind" as I am today— and going to Gibbons was definitely the start of that very important process.

THE BREAKDOWN:
PART FOUR

BACK TO BOSTON

I COULDN'T PUT IT OFF ANY LONGER. It was time to report to training camp back in Boston. But I was in no way, shape, or form ready to play.

Let's start with the shape. Even though I had bulked up to more than 200 pounds for my second season with the Celtics so I could be as powerful as possible on the court, when it finally came time to report to training camp, I was down to 184 pounds. No good.

I had lost almost twenty pounds in fourteen days. My appetite was still completely gone. Whatever my problems were, they were all internal—even though those problems were now manifesting themselves in my external appearance.

The sad part was that I had really enjoyed the previous year playing with the Celtics, and I was looking forward to coming back for more. I was grateful they were bringing me in for a second season, because, as most of you reading this know, the Boston Celtics are one of the great teams of pro basketball. It was an honor to play for them.

But the way I was feeling, I couldn't play for *nobody*.

At the time, the coach of the Celtics was the legendary "Doc" Rivers, who, ironically, is now with the first NBA team I ever played for, the L.A. Clippers. He, too, had been a point guard in the NBA during his playing days, so I felt he really understood me. To me, he was like an uncle I could trust with almost anything. As a matter of fact, I soon would be trusting him with my very life.

Because he had been so good to me, I knew I owed Doc the truth about my condition. So, when I got to training camp, I went straight to his office and said, "Doc, I don't know what's going on with me. Something happened to me—I don't know what exactly, but I've got to try to get to the bottom of it. But right now, I just don't feel like I can play, Doc."

To my relief, he was incredibly supportive.

"Whatever you need," were the first words out of his mouth. "If you need time away, just take some time off and come back when you're ready—you don't have to retire. You don't have to do that.

"Or…if you really feel like you do need to retire, that's your decision. Whatever you need to do, we're going to be behind you and get you whatever you need— because I love ya. We just want to make sure you're okay, because you've got so much to give."

But because I was only sharing so much about what was really going on with me, he could only do so much for me. Retirement was still in my head; the low shot clock was still ticking down. I felt so much pressure inside that it seemed like retirement was the only way to relieve it.

WHAT'S DRIVING YOU???

I would be proven wrong about that—but at that point, I was just after a quick and easy answer that would bring me some instant relief.

Next, Doc and I got together with the Celtics' president of basketball operations, Danny Ainge. I told Danny how I was feeling and he, too, showed his heart to me, just as Doc did. He had been a player and he and Doc shared some of the difficult personal challenges they had gone through, so I would know these kinds of crisis points happen with players. He also told me that we would work things out, however I wanted things to go.

You hear a lot about how cold and ruthless the professional sports world can be. Sure, I've seen that side of it—but on that day, I was so grateful for these two men and their caring and understanding of my situation. Danny even came to the home I was renting for myself and my family in Boston and sat down with me and my wife.

In my mind, I know that the Celtics organization would truly do their best to do what was best for me. Even though things were about to get incredibly dark, I at least knew way down deep that they would continue to have my back.

But the unthinkable was about to become reality. I talked about what I should do with everyone in my closest circle, everyone I trusted at the time. But I knew I was going through the motions. The decision had already been made way down deep inside of me. I knew it was over.

I was done with playing basketball. Forever.

TRAVELING

SUMMERTIME WAS WHEN I REALLY GOT OUT of the hood and went places. Places I had never seen before.

I told you about the neighborhood travel team I had played on until I was fourteen. That was an awesome experience. But when you start playing high school ball, if you're good enough, you get to step up to a whole other level of summer travel teams. These aren't teams just made up of kids from around where you live—these are teams made up of kids from all over your state—and you get to play in *national* tournaments.

To the general public, these basketball teams and tournaments are known as Amateur Athletic Union (AAU) programs, but the AAU itself isn't actually attached to as many of these programs as they used to be. In the 90s, different companies began sponsoring these programs on their own. On the west coast, Nike sponsored most of the events and on the east coast, it was Adidas.

You only had to take one look at me in those days to

know who I was playing my summer basketball for—because a lot of the time, I was wearing Adidas from head to toe. Obviously, one awesome perk of being on an Adidas-sponsored team is they gave you a lot of their gear.

But playing on these kinds of teams wasn't about getting new sneakers (although, considering our financial situation, those sneakers were definitely appreciated). The fact was, these summer tournaments were a young player's opportunity to get national exposure, usually for the first time. We would be scouted and ranked. This was crucial to my ultimate plan of getting a basketball scholarship to a good college.

The first summer I played for an Adidas team, the Florida Flash, was the one between my freshman and sophomore years at Gibbons. I almost didn't make it on the team—once again, the powers-that-be didn't think I was good enough. Two buddies of mine who were invited to be on the team went to bat for me, however. They said my stats from Gibbons didn't tell the whole story—so I got my slot.

That meant that I got to train in Princeton, New Jersey at the NBA Players Association camp. And it also meant I got to go to Las Vegas for the actual tournament. Vegas was cool, even though it was really, really, really hot—nothing like being out in the desert in the summer. But it was awesome to finally see with your own eyes what you've been seeing on TV all your life.

Best of all, I was playing with and against the best of the best at basketball in my age group. Not too long before this, Kobe Bryant had come up through this tournament as had Kevin Garnett. Tracy McGrady, who went right into the

NBA out of high school, was one of my teammates on the Flash. It was a good place to be if you wanted the decision makers to see what you could do on the court.

It was very competitive. Our team did well, and we all performed at a high level, but we didn't win the championship that year (or the next summer, when I played with the Flash again).

But I achieved the result I wanted. After the first summer with the Adidas team, I was ranked among the top fifty players in the country. After the second summer? I was ranked in the top fifteen.

I can't tell you how satisfying it was to be mentioned in the same breath with the elite high school players in all of America, especially when I almost didn't make the team in the first place. As I've said, though, I never let other people's judgments of my abilities stop me.

The funny thing was, even as my reputation was growing by leaps and bounds nationally, it was sinking back in my old neighborhood! Because I had gone to Gibbons, everybody back home stopped paying attention to me. They weren't coming to see me play, so nobody was talking about me.

But soon they would be. Sooner than even I expected.

THE HOME TEAM

I HAD CHANGED BY THE TIME I reached my junior year at Cardinal Gibbons. That change was dramatic and for the better.

For one thing, I had found my social game at school. I knew who was my friend and who wasn't—so I learned how to fit in. I would even party with some of the kids. These get-togethers were different than the ones in the hood. Believe it or not, these kids would use harder drugs than my neighborhood friends did; the most we would do back home was smoke some weed. I guess they had more money and could afford to party a lot harder than my old buddies could!

The other big change was in my body. When I started as a freshman, I was only about five feet, seven inches tall. I made it to about five feet, nine inches at the end of that season. As a sophomore, I added another two inches, then, finally, my junior year, I hit six feet, three inches. That's when my physical development took off, because I really started working to make myself as strong as possible. I quit smoking and drinking. I started running down the beach and running in the pool—and in both cases, I did it with my shoes on. I did a lot of push-ups and played a lot more bball. And I put a lot more into my study of the game. I watched games all day long when I could to make sure I was as sharp mentally as I was physically when I came out on the court.

Academically, I had grown tremendously as well. When I started at Gibbons, I can't even remember how long it took me to do my homework; it just seemed endless. Now, I was nailing it every night in thirty or forty minutes.

Back in the hood, things continued to go well with my relationship with Tosha. I was also beginning to be recognized there as a player to be reckoned with again. I had more time after school, since I was able to do my homework so much faster. That meant I was able to play a lot more on the local courts. People saw how big I had become and how my skills had developed. Finally, some respect was coming back my way from my own people.

I had come a long way from that kid in ninth grade, struggling with relearning my position as point guard, trying to boost a 1.5 GPA, and feeling out of sorts both at my new school and in my old community. Now, my confidence was high, I was in peak physical condition, I had upped my academic game, and I had an incredible relationship with Tosha.

Not only that, but, because of the exposure I got from my summers playing for the Adidas teams, colleges were already starting to recruit me—the important next step of my own personal game plan. That process began when I was a sophomore. I saw legendary college basketball coach Rick Pitino in the stands once when I was playing, checking us out—and he had recently taken the Kentucky Wildcats to an NCAA championship. A lot of influential people came to our games at that time to scout Major Parker—but they saw me playing too, and that put me on their radar.

All of these factors gave me a new sense of security about my future. That, in turn, fueled my desire to finish my high school career back where I started—in my own community at Dillard High.

Even though I had overcome the many challenges I had faced at Gibbons, I knew inside I still didn't feel entirely comfortable there, practicing and playing with our basketball team. Yes, by that time, I was pretty popular with the teachers and the other kids—especially since I did so well with the basketball team. Yes, people knew colleges were recruiting me and I was regarded as an asset at the school.

But there was still an element there that would not look past my background and my skin color. It continued to be difficult for me to deal with on a day-to-day basis. And, in the spring of my junior year, an incident involving that element would cause me to jump schools months before I had planned.

A girl passing by me in the hall, with a group of her friends, yelled to me in a loud voice, "OH! WASSUP MY NIGGA! WASSUP MY NIGGA!"

This was not the first time something like this had happened to me. I knew it was the kind of situation where she had turned to her friends when she saw me approaching and said to them, "I'm going to call him a n— and laugh!"

This was, however, the first time that I didn't get *angry* about getting called that name by kids trying to score points with their posse. No, in a way I felt grateful— because I had been itching to go back to Dillard and now I had the perfect excuse. No one would question my motives; everyone knew what had happened. Now I had the opportunity to go to the same school as Tosha, play ball with my old middle school teammates, and finish my schooling with the kids I started out with.

So I didn't create a lot of drama. The next day, April 10, 1997, I simply transferred back to Dillard. It was such a big deal it made the newspaper—the headline of the story read, "Top Guard Transfers to Dillard." My quote this time was all my own words—"I pretty much felt like I always be-longed at Dillard." And that was the truth.

As for the girl who had said this to me, the rest of her high school experience after that incident wasn't so good. My teammates were livid that she had driven me from the school and almost got suspended for their behavior against her; that's how close those kids and I were. I felt bad about leaving that team behind, but I knew this was the best move for me and exactly how I wanted to end my playing career in Fort Lauderdale.

Back at Dillard, my senior year was everything I hoped it would be and more—truly an awesome time. The community really came together behind our Dillard team and I felt like we had inspired a lot of people with our level of play. We made it to the state final four, just as our team had at Gibbons two out of the three years I played for them.

Not only that, but academically, I made all As without a sweat. Once again, I saw the huge gulf between the quality of education I had experienced at a private school and a public school. Suddenly, I didn't have to really do homework anymore. I was just able to get great grades because I had such a high level of training at Gibbons—and so little was expected at Dillard. I could only wish that everyone in my community could have benefited from the educational opportunities I had been blessed with.

My senior year at Dillard was like a big warm hug from all the people I loved and who loved me. Coming back erased any lingering resentment that came from those who felt my choice to go to Cardinal Gibbons was some kind of betrayal. They say you can't go home again, but I did—and I was glad I had.

But I couldn't stay there if I was going to fulfill my NBA dream. And that meant a lot more challenges, a lot more work, and a lot more radical adjustments to new situations where I wouldn't be the most comfortable.

I had a sneak peek at one of those uncomfortable situations when my future college coach showed up in the hood to recruit me and one of my Dillard teammates. He was the only one brave enough to come down there to talk to me and the other guy he was interested in. It was quite a scene—this grizzled sixty-plus-year-old white guy, walking through the projects like he owned the place, facing down a pit bull sitting outside in the yard. The guy didn't flinch. He put out his hand, patted the dog's head and said to us, "Look at this pretty thing." He would be one of the toughest men I would ever encounter—and more than a few sparks were going to fly between us.

But that old man wasn't my primary concern my freshman year at college. *My* old man was.

JUMP BALL

I CAME HOME FROM THE SEATTLE-L.A. charity trip feeling exhausted and dehydrated. I wasn't eating, I wasn't sleeping, and I was still grappling with the dark visions that kept invading my head.

I had barely arrived for my freshman year at the University at Missouri when the unthinkable happened.

My Pop had a serious stroke.

I had to immediately go home and see what was happening and how he was doing. I couldn't conceive of my dad going down like that. To me, it was like hearing Superman couldn't get off the ground. I was terrified. Suddenly, the man I had always looked up to was down, a man who never ran out of words now couldn't speak.

It was low shot clock time again.

Not only was I incredibly concerned for his health, but now I had to think about stepping up ASAP to be the family breadwinner. As I said, our folks' finances were already strained to the max—they could even lose their house. If I couldn't earn in the NBA, I didn't know what was going to happen to my mom and dad— not to mention me.

That meant I had to make my mark fast playing ball for the Missouri Tigers. That also meant I was about to butt heads with one of the most respected coaches in college basketball, a guy who was starting his 32nd year coaching "Mizzou," the nickname for the school.

Yeah, that was the same guy who came to the hood and faced down a pit bull. Now, it was my turn, and the interaction would not be as friendly as it was with that dog in the projects.

A few months before that, I was on an incredible high. After I graduated from Dillard, I was given an awesome opportunity—to play on the 1998 USA Men's Junior World Championship Qualifying Team. This team was backed by the organization that selected the US Olympic basketball team and put together the legendary 1992 "Dream Team," which contained what has been called the greatest collection of basketball talent ever assembled, with such amazing athletes as Michael Jordan, Magic Johnson, Larry Bird, Patrick Ewing, and Charles Barkley playing together for the first time.

I had to go to the US Olympic training center in Colorado Springs, Colorado to try out against the best players in the country in my age group. I had to give it my all, and I did; I made the cut. Our team, which contained my future Clippers teammate Quentin Richardson, then got to travel to the Dominican Republic for the international tournament. Under the leadership of Syracuse coach Jim Boeheim, we won the gold medal in early July, going 6-0 against teams from Argentina, Brazil, Canada, and other countries in the Americas. I was proud to have been a starter in each one of those games.

My first international tournament also provided me with another important glimpse into another culture. This time, I was exposed to a people who were living in extreme poverty like nothing I had seen in the hood. There was beautiful scenery and incredible resources in the Dominican Republic—but most of the people living there had nothing. The police force kept a firm grip on the population, walking around holding rifles, while children were forced to beg for money and food. That gave me some perspective.

Speaking of cultures, I also got to see just how special the rest of the world thought America was. Players for the other teams would always want to trade T-shirts and stuff for things from their countries, which I was happy to do. For me, it was awesome to get some swag from Argentina or whatever place another team was from.

All in all, being on the USA team was another great broadening experience for a kid from the hood. These kinds of experiences always nourished my spirit and helped me to develop a more enlightened viewpoint toward the entire world and my place in it.

But that enjoyable interlude was over, and I had to start thinking about how I was going to make my mark in NCAA basketball. I had ended up at the University of Missouri because of two factors—one of my Dillard teammates was going to go there with me and, once again, I would be allowed to play varsity basketball immediately. I was very conscious about remaining as visible as possible so I would have a chance to build my national reputation, just as my travel teams in the past had.

I had been heavily recruited my senior year of high school and had been flown out to visit several colleges. There was one southern college where I remember feeling very uncomfortable—I saw a few Confederate flags on campus and didn't want to be around that kind of culture, especially after my experiences at Cardinal Gibbons.

But Mizzou was another story. They flew me to St. Louis, and then put me on a private plane to go the university, which is located about halfway between St. Louis and Kansas City, Missouri. We got to go to one of their football games and also party with some guys I knew from the Adidas teams I had played against years before.

And, as I said, Norm Stewart was the only coach to actually come into the hood to talk to us. Missouri was very persistent; the people there gave me a good feeling that this was a place that would allow me to show off my skills.

Now, a little more about Norm Stewart. Here were some of his accomplishments from his more than three decades of coaching Mizzou basketball:

- Eight Big Eight Conference regular-season championships
- Six Big Eight Conference postseason tournament titles
- Sixteen NCAA Tournament appearances, including two Elite Eights
- 1982 UPI National Coach Of The Year and 1994 Associated Press Coach of the Year
- Lifetime record of 728-374

WHAT'S DRIVING YOU???

- Seventeen seasons with twenty wins or more
- Coached nine All-American players and twenty-one First-Team All-Conference players

Ultimately, "Stormin' Norman," his nickname at the college, would be responsible for more than 60 percent of the basketball wins over the school's entire history!

With my dad sick and my family needing money, I started the season with my low shot clock mindset. I felt like I was battling time, that I couldn't afford to wait; I had to play amazing ball on the court and I had to do it NOW.

That meant I was much, much, much more concerned with my future than my coach's past. Part of me just wanted to have an incredible breakout year on the court, and then go right into the NBA draft at the end of my freshman year. This wasn't my original plan; I just felt an enormous pressure to start making that NBA salary as soon as I could.

Look, I'm aware of the need to keep college sports as clean as possible—but the fact is, on an annual basis, tens of millions of dollars are coming into the top schools from their basketball programs (more than $100 million to the cream of the crop) and coaches are getting million-dollar-plus salaries. Meanwhile, there are players like me, who come into college as broke as they come, left struggling.

Granted, my case was extraordinary—suddenly, my family needed me to provide —but, then again, it wasn't. Many athletes are from the kind of poor areas I grew up in and also have families depending on them. That's a big part of what drives them—and what was driving me. Much of the public doesn't understand that pressure and what it can do to you, especially when you're producing for the college and struggling to get enough to eat at the same time.

But the NCAA rules are so strict that even working to make some extra cash became difficult. One of the sponsors of the basketball program owned a big restaurant/bar off campus that was extremely popular. He hired me to work for him to help me out in the summers, but I had to be careful about accepting anything more than a job from him. A free burger was even questionable, but many a night after eight o'clock, when the school mess hall had closed, I ran down there for something to eat. It was awesome, but could've possibly gotten me and him in trouble.

Now, you might ask, wasn't room and board part of my scholarship package? It most definitely was, but when you're a serious athlete, you can't get by on what a typical student eats. You're burning some serious energy and you have to keep strong—so that means a lot of food.

One thing I would always try to do to save money was, at the beginning of the weekend, I would make a big pot of spaghetti and fry some wings, buffalo-style. For two or three days, we'd eat that food. I'd also buy hamburger meat, sandwich meat and sausages—maybe I didn't know George Foreman personally, but his grill sure was our best friend at college.

College to a lot of people just meant a nonstop party, interrupted by some classes from time to time. For me and the other players, it was an exhausting experience. To be honest with you, being poor at college was a lot harder than when I was poor at home.

Here was a typical day during the preseason. You had to

be at the practice facility at five-thirty in the morning and get in an hour-and-fifteen-minute workout where you really had to push yourself. After that, a quick breakfast and then, maybe, at eight o'clock, your classes would start. At one o'clock, you'd have individual workouts, at three o'clock, weightlifting. At five o'clock, study hall. This was all strictly enforced, so you *had* to do it.

And man, it is *hard*. It is very hard, and then you're broke on top of that. So you learn to enjoy little things like just being able to play video games for an hour or so or hanging out with people.

At first, though, I didn't want to hang out with anybody except my teammates. I was very standoffish with the rest of the students because of what I had gone through at Cardinal Gibbons. People knew who I was, because my arrival was heavily publicized. They approached me in a friendly way, but I felt like they only wanted to hang out with me because I was a hot All-American basketball recruit.

I never liked that kind of attention and still don't.

I responded to people who liked me for who I was, not what I accomplished. So I kept to myself at the beginning. If anything, I tried to dress as thuggish as possible to keep the phonies away from me. I was consciously pushing people away instead of giving them a chance to know me on a real level.

Sometimes, however, you build up walls inside yourself that you just don't need. As a matter of fact, they get in the way of fully enjoying life.

My teammates, God bless them, they broke me down and pulled me out into the social scene. They ended up really helping me change my perspective, because they loved me for who I was, not for how well I played. We were all from different backgrounds and I really got close to not only them, but their families as well. Thanks to my buddies, I had a lot of new experiences. They took me sledding and I saw snow for the first time. I even did my first tailgate party. I also became friends with a guy who was from a family of billionaires, somebody I never could have imagined palling around with.

But *only* a little.

Above all else, I wanted to become a great basketball player. I *needed* to become a great basketball player. The strict physical regimen did its job. I had never had my body worked that hard, but I knew it was responding, so I felt good about the training even if I didn't feel so good about my finances. Again, I was determined to make good—*fast*. I felt I had to.

But Stormin' Norman had a different timetable for me.

ONE·ON·ONE

A BIG REASON I WENT TO CARDNIAL GIBBONS was to play varsity basketball on day one. Same with Mizzou. But, when the season started, I didn't find myself playing much.

Why? Norm Stewart.

Norm was in his 32nd and final season of coaching college ball. I was playing my first. He rightly thought I needed a little seasoning—but the way he went about doing it almost drove me to leave the program.

All coaches have different styles to try and make you a better player. But there are what I call old school coaches and new school coaches, and Coach Stewart was definitely old school.

What defines an old school coach in my mind? Well, he's more like a drill sergeant from the military. He's tough, he's even mean, he doesn't back away from telling you what you're doing wrong in gruesome detail, and he'll bust you down. Now, he has a reason for tearing you down—it's so that he can build you right back up.

I was once again expected to rise up to a new level of bball, just as I had been expected to at Cardinal Gibbons— and Coach Stewart was determined to get me there, in his old school way. He started telling me I couldn't shoot. Over and over again. And he stopped playing me as much as I should have been playing over this "issue."

During one game we were playing in Colorado, he took me out of the game and yelled at his assistant coach, "You tell your Florida All-American NOT to shoot the ball!" Of course, I heard that loud and clear—the message was really directed at me. But I was determined to prove him wrong. I was gonna show him I could go to the hole as good as anybody. As you know from reading my story up to this point, I never let anyone set a limit on what my abilities were.

So…the second he put me back in the game, I went ahead and shot the ball.

To say the least, he didn't react well to that. I immediately got benched for the rest of the game. That was a bitter pill to swallow, so bitter I couldn't get it down. I had a breakdown on the bench. I actually cried and said to myself, "You know what? I'm out of here. He doesn't see my talent. He said I would have an opportunity to play and I'm just sitting here." I was losing my confidence rapidly and I felt desperate about my situation at the same time.

Basketball, to me, was my ticket to get my family out of the hood and I was not about to let this man stop me. I was playing hard because I wanted to be "one and done"—and go for the NBA after my freshman year. Maybe I was playing too hard for that reason. However, I felt like I had a coach who didn't believe in me at a moment when I needed one that did, desperately.

After the game, I said, "Hey listen, I'm transferring. This isn't working out for me. I'll go somewhere else and show you how good I am."

A couple days went by and we were able to work out our differences. In fact, I started the next game. And when we reached the second half of the season, my game really took off. I saw a lot more game time and had a lot of fun on the court.

In the end, our team went 20 and 9 and we made it to the first round of the NCAA tournament. And I was proud to be named to the Big 12 Conference All-Freshman team for the 1998-99 season.

Coach Stewart made me a tougher player. Looking back on it, I see that the things about him that made me so angry actually helped make my career; he did in fact break me down to build me back up, better and stronger than I had been before.

I also finally learned that the game wasn't just about my physical skills—it was about my mental ones as well.

That understanding came about because of a class I took in sports psychology. I connected strongly with everything I learned in that class; it was the first time I had the things I felt inside explained to me in a way that made sense. More importantly, the class gave me many useful and valuable tools that helped me immediately understand what I was going through with Stormin' Norman—and would continue helping me all throughout my career.

I learned how to visualize and use other mental

techniques that would help me deal with the anxiety that comes with having to consistently perform at a high level. I also learned how to organize my approach to the game, and take on new memory systems that helped me instinctively know the right way to deal with all kinds of game situations.

Overall, the class really inspired me—and completely changed the way I viewed sports from a purely physical thing to something that utilized my brain as well as my body.

Of course, the whole idea of a "mental game" wasn't new. There were always talks from my father and different coaches through the years about how I needed to be mentally tough and think positive on the court. But those talks were a lot more simplistic—these guys weren't psychologists. They knew your head should be in the right place, but they couldn't exactly tell you how to get it there!

Now, for the first time, I understood how my mind worked under stress and was given practical approaches to empower my thought processes. Instead of being *told* about the mental aspect of the game, I was *taught* about how it functions and how I could control it.

Big difference.

You can be educated about something, but it doesn't mean anything until you've had the *education,* if you know what I mean. For example, a coach might say you need to change your diet to get more muscular. But if that coach (or somebody else) never tells you exactly *how* to change your diet—what you should be eating and how much and what you should avoid—you don't know where to start if you don't already have that knowledge base. So it's a whole lot tougher to achieve the result you want.

WHAT'S DRIVING YOU???

I've learned through the years that whatever you want to accomplish in life, it's crucial to have a game plan in place to reach your goal. And now, when it came to my mental game, I finally had one.

So overall, my freshman year of college was a powerful one for me, filled with a lot of great progress both on and off the court. Plus, my father had largely recovered from his stroke within a few months; the only sign of ongoing damage was the fact that his speech was still slightly slurred. He and my brother were working again, so the financial situation wasn't quite as desperate.

That meant the pressure was off as far as my needing to try for the NBA after my freshman year—I knew it wasn't the right time for me. Now I had another season to get myself ready.

However, I was at a crossroads at the end of the season.

I was still thinking about transferring to another school. I spent a few weeks considering the possibilities—but finally decided I should stick it out. I wanted to get back on the court and prove myself once and for all to Coach Stewart.

Turned out I didn't have to. After my personal decision, he made one of his own—*he* was retiring.

I want to make it clear that I definitely appreciate what Norm Stewart did for me, especially at this point in my life, when I can look back at the lessons I learned and how important they were to my overall development.

But, at *that* point in my life? To be honest, I appreciated that there was going to be a coaching change!

TIME-OUT

WE ALL FACE PRESSURE POINTS IN OUR LIVES.

My first year at Missouri was one of those points. My Pop was down for the count and I felt the family was depending on me to succeed. Meanwhile, Coach Stewart, while he was trying to make me a better player, also caused me to briefly lose my confidence and my hope because of his whole approach to the process.

This was far from the worst year of my life—and I'm not talking about the year I had my breakdown either. But it *was* another year that challenged me in dramatic ways, toughened me up, and tested my resilience.

What I've learned from these pressure points is that you can't let them break you. You have to have the strength to find your way out.

For example, sometimes a situation just presents an overwhelming challenge, where the answer isn't right there in front of you and you're not sure what do to next. When that happens, the solution is to look for the tools and the people who can help you meet that challenge.

Take academics. Any inner-city kid like me was going to have trouble transitioning to a posh private school like Cardinal Gibbons. I had to understand that my initial difficulties weren't a question of my intelligence—it was a question of my training (or, to be clear, my *lack* of training). Once I had that training, it served me well through the rest of high school and college. It still serves me today as I strive to learn everything I need to know to achieve my current goals.

On the other hand, sometimes you find yourself banging up against other people's judgments of you—judgments that may limit or diminish you, even though those judgments have nothing to do with your reality.

When it came to basketball, I often arrived at a place where somebody told me I wasn't good enough or where the powers-that-be didn't see me as a starter or a varsity player. I had two choices: I could either accept their verdict or show them they were wrong. I always chose the latter course, by continuing to grow and improve, and also, when necessary, simply choosing to play somewhere else where I *would* be appreciated.

These situations weren't about me being big-headed or egotistical. It was a question of me knowing my capabilities when others didn't. I had goals that I wanted to achieve and that I knew I could achieve. I just had to find the right opportunities to prove myself. Again, rejection is redirection.

Pressure points make us grow. They force us to improve our abilities, sharpen our mindsets, and find deeper levels of commitment that help us realize our dreams. I wouldn't have made it to the NBA without my pressure points.

I'm grateful for them.

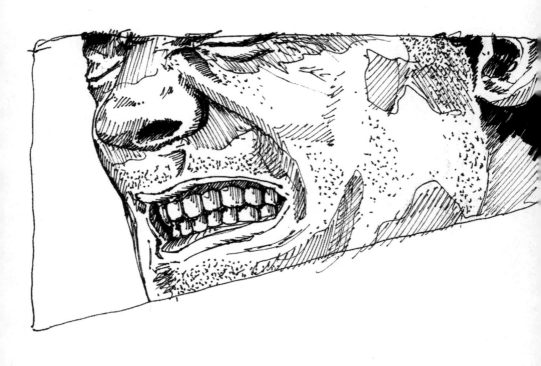

THE BREAKDOWN:
PART FIVE

TEAMWORK

THE CELTICS WERE WAITING ON ME for my final decision about retiring. I knew I wanted to quit—but thinking about it just sparked massive panic attacks inside me. I continued to feel like everything was out of control.

My teammates instantly knew something was wrong, because I wasn't acting like my usual self. Guys I had been mentoring, like Rajon Rondo and Avery Bradley, suddenly were looking after me, because I was thinking I was going to die; I was thinking the low shot clock was finally running out, I was lost, and I was scared. Avery was especially concerned, since he had been on the trip to Seattle with me and had actually witnessed the start of my breakdown.

One night, I went over to Avery's house, because I really didn't know what was going on inside my head. I needed some space and he welcomed me into his home. His mother-in-law even tried to help me—she jumped on Skype because they had somebody in their family who'd gone through something like what I was experiencing, so she wanted to see if that person could help.

A lot of this period is still a blur to me, but I do know that everybody only wanted good things for me and tried to do everything they could for me. Not just Danny, not just Doc, not just my teammates, but all their families as well. Everybody was worried about me and everybody wanted to see me come through this okay.

The day I went in to tell Danny Ainge that I was quitting for sure, I had my son, KJ, with me. He was just under three years old at that time and there was no way he should've been alone with me in my state, even though I seemed okay when I left with him. Tosha instantly felt something wasn't right after I left; she called Rondo and Avery, telling them, "Listen, just go get him. Go get him and my son."

It was a good thing she did.

Because, I felt another huge panic attack coming at me as I was in Danny's office, about to tell him I was retiring for sure. I don't even remember if that was the day I did tell him or not, I only know that, as I lost control of my thoughts, BOOM!, Avery and Rondo were suddenly there to take my son from me, protect him from me, and protect me from myself.

As they drove me home, I really fell apart. I suddenly thought it was my job to bring everybody to Jesus, right that second, when I was the guy who needed the saving. Yep, I was cracking up. I started calling everyone I knew and loved, exclaiming loudly over the phone to them, "We've got to come to Christ!" On the other side of the call, I would hear them say to whoever was around them, "Oh, he's crazy, he lost it!"

WHAT'S DRIVING YOU???

Luckily for me, poor Avery, bless his heart, did not lose it. He stayed poised and strong and determined. All my teammates did, especially Chris Wilcox, Rondo, and Avery. You could not tell those three men that I was out of my mind. They were like, "No, KD's straight. He's just going through something; he'll be all right."

They were there for me. And I thank God they were.

SLAM DUNK

AFTER THE BASKETBALL SEASON, as my freshman college year was winding down, I was honored to once again be asked to try out for the USA Junior World Championship Team—and I was good enough to make the team again.

And like before, the experience was everything I could want. The previous year, I had gotten to go to a Yankees game with the rest of the team, stay at Syracuse U., and get coached by the legendary Jim Boeheim (now in his 38th year coaching the Syracuse Orange team). This year, we were coached by Rob Evans from Arizona State. In both cases, I got to stay in different parts of the country and meet (and even party with) different and amazing people along the way. It's the biggest dream you can imagine for somebody who wanted, above all else, to be a pro basketball player.

This time, the location of the actual tournament, held once again in July, was a lot further than the Dominican Republic; I got to travel to Portugal. Another difference? This time, we got beat!

The previous year had been a tournament only of the Americas, which meant we played teams from Canada, South America, and Central America. This year, it was a global tournament—and suddenly we were up against China, Russia, and Egypt, among other countries.

No problem, right? Basketball was America's game, right?

Well, we were shocked to see the level of play from some of these other countries. Evidently the Michael Jordan 1992 Dream Team had not only inspired us—but them as well!

Even so, we breezed through most of the tournament with victory after victory after victory. We had six in a row, just like the previous year. This time around, however, there was a seventh all-important game, the final against Spain. That game was brutally close; I dunked with twenty seconds left in the game to bring us within three points, but they came back just as quickly to take us for a final score of 94-87.

Portugal was memorable because, first of all, I could legally have a drink there. The drinking age was eighteen and I was nineteen. Secondly, I could have that drink at a bullfight. So there I was, in Lisbon at a bullfight, with a beautiful view of the ocean beyond the arena, being a little surprised at watching what actually *happens* at a bullfight. Meaning, after the bull rushes past the matador, the matador immediately starts stabbing the bull. Not what I'd call a fair fight!

But it was still a magical moment. I had to take stock of how far I had come already in my young life. I was a kid from the hood, enjoying a bullfight in Lisbon, who had gotten to play in an international tournament with the world's best basketball players in my age group. Seven or eight of the players that were in the tournament would go on to the NBA, including Andrei Kirilenko from the Russian team and Pau Gasol from Spain.

I felt good being in their company—and knowing I could play at their level.

After that experience, it was back to reality. Because I couldn't count on making the NBA after my sophomore year, I spent most of the summer in Missouri, taking a business management course specifically targeted at the restaurant/bar and wholesale industries. Like my father and the sponsor who helped me out at Missouri with a summer job, I wanted to know how to run a successful business if basketball didn't work out for me. I had to cover all my bases.

There was another situation I had to address—Tosha. During my freshman year, between my dad's stroke and my difficult time under Norm Stewart, I couldn't handle the responsibilities of a long-distance relationship. So...I had broken it off with Natosha with a quick and cold phone call. I couldn't really deal with any kind of prolonged, painful discussion.

What it really came down to was, I was still very young and I was still figuring out who I was. I also wanted to have a little fun and have something to compare that relationship to, so I could be sure about my future.

Now I was.

Tosha had just graduated high school and was making plans to go to college at Florida State University (FSU) in Tallahassee. I was back for a short period during the summer and I wrote her a letter, saying something like, "I know we broke up, but I'm back at home now, I'd like to see you and see where things go."

Lucky for me, she agreed to take me back.

We became closer than ever, and maintained that closeness during my sophomore year back in Missouri. But that made the physical distance between us even harder to deal with. So we decided, no matter what, the following year we would be together. She would come to whatever city I ended up in. After this year, there would be no more separation.

We would be together. As we are to this day.

With that taken care of, it was time to march through the final steps toward my NBA dream. That meant I needed to have a great season at Mizzou and I needed the recognition that would put me on the radar of the NBA draft— because my sophomore year of college was going to be my last. I was determined that 2000 would be the year I would make it to the pros.

The Team USA experiences, together with my development playing under Norm Stewart, combined to create a quantum leap in my bball skills going into my sophomore year. Even though I wasn't regarded as one of the top college point guards, I felt in my heart I was—and that confidence propelled me into one last great season at Missouri.

Adding to that confidence was what my new coach, Quin Snyder, would bring to my skills. This would be his first of seven years at Missouri; prior to this, he had been assistant coach of the Los Angeles Lakers, as well as at Duke University for six years. He had worked with two amazing organizations, and, in his first position as head coach, he had the opportunity to put what he had learned to work.

WHAT'S DRIVING YOU???

I benefited from his youth, his energy, and his knowledge. He, too, took me to another level of game play, but in a more positive way than Coach Stewart had. Mentally, he fired up my confidence, and physically, he changed my stroke and worked on having me shoot without jumping so high.

Still, I often took flight on court. As a matter of fact, one of my flying dunks at Mizzou is ranked as one of the top 100 moments of that school's basketball history; if you google "Keyon Dooling and the greatest dunk that never happened," you'll find the video—you'll also see a freeze-frame of my shocked expression when a foul was called on me for charging! That expression was so memorable that the guy who did these Missouri posts wrote, *"If I ever change my handle name, it will be 'Keyon Dooling's Shock Face.'"*

Coach Snyder spent a lot of one-on-one time helping me continue to improve. He was a very good communicator, very emotional, and very passionate. Ultimately, I benefited from his style of play more than from Norm Stewart's, but both men were equally important to my development. Coach Snyder brought the team back to the first round of the NCAA tournament and he was recognized as Rookie Coach of the Year by *The Basketball Times*.

As for me, I was a unanimous second-team all-Big 12 selection that season. I led the team in scoring (15.3 per game), assists (3.7 per game) and blocked shots (17). I actually came close to doubling my scoring average from my freshman year.

But that didn't mean all my problems in life had been magically solved. While I had a much more enjoyable experience on the basketball court, my sophomore year was still clouded by the fact that I was broke—and back home in Fort Lauderdale, my family was fast running out of funds.

Yes, I had a lot of students giving me shout-outs on campus and looking up to me. Unfortunately, after they'd tell me how great I was, I'd watch them drive off in a shiny new car and I'd be left standing there with basically nothing to my name.

It was difficult. I can't lie.

A sports star always gets a lot of attention and accolades, but, in college, that's all that a sports star gets. And when you're scraping to get by, and you know your parents have it even tougher than you, you can't relax and enjoy the attention. You have to keep achieving, you have to keep moving forward, and you have to plan out just how you're going to start earning serious money ASAP.

My internal low shot clock was counting down again; I knew I couldn't afford to spend another year playing college ball, even though the experience might further develop my skills. I knew I was good enough for the pros—and I knew I couldn't wait. It was time to make my move.

So in April, when basketball season was done, so was I. On April 21, with Coach Snyder by my side, I declared my eligibility for the NBA draft. My quote for the school newspaper was this:

> "This was a tough decision to make, but I feel that it's in my best interests right now to enter the draft. It's a dream of mine to play in the NBA, and I believe I have an opportunity to realize

that at this point in time. I love the University of
Missouri, and I'm very proud of what my teammates and I accomplished this year. I learned so
much this year playing for Coach Snyder. As for
the last few weeks, I want to thank everyone for
their support."

Now I only had two months to prepare. Two months to
realize my ultimate ambition.

June 28, 2000 was the date of that year's NBA draft. And
I was going to be as ready as possible—even if I had to go
into debt to do it.

GOALTENDING

WHAT'S MORE EXHILARATING THAN BEING two months away from seeing your dream become reality?

And what's more terrifying than not knowing if that dream will actually come true?

The stakes, of course, were enormous. Once I declared for the draft, I couldn't go back and play college ball because of the NCAA rules prohibiting it. My future options would be severely limited if the draft didn't happen for me.

Not only that, I wasn't seen at that time as a big deal by the NBA. I was mostly on their radar because of my accomplishments on the USA teams during the previous two summers.

The top college players had been at the Colorado Springs tryouts for the USA team. Most of the guys had bigger names and were at more high-profile basketball programs than Missouri's. Many also would be, in the future, headed to the NBA, including Kenyon Martin, who would be the number one pick in the 2000 draft, as well as other now-familiar pro names such as Shawn Marion, Wally Szczerbiak, Troy Murphy, Quentin Richardson, Rip Hamilton, and Steve Blake. When you have that much talent under one tent, there are also, naturally, a lot of people scouting that talent.

That's why I saw it as a chance to shine.

I had played my heart out during those tryouts and it paid off. Even though I was around all these other college kids who were much more well-known than I was, I had been told the second time I played for the USA team, that I was the best overall point guard of the group.

Since I had tested myself against the best and come away with that positive verdict, I knew I had what it takes to excel in the draft. But I still had to raise my profile high enough to get ranked high and picked early. And, again, I had two months to make that happen.

I went to Atlanta, Georgia to begin my training and Tosha came with me. From this point on, we were determined to fulfill our promise to live together no matter what happened. I told her, "No matter where I'm going, baby, I want you with me. You've got to be with me, you've got to be here. We can do this. I want you in my life." Distance had always been too hard on our relationship and I didn't want anything threatening what we had. It also gave me the stability I needed as I pursued the draft.

As I trained, I worked with Craig Neal, an NBA scout at the time. I was in Atlanta for about a month, working out for about fifteen or sixteen teams, I can't even remember how many. I just remember it was constant and I was giving 100 percent, because my entire future was on the line.

WHAT'S DRIVING YOU???

You might be asking, "Well, if you and your family were so broke, how in the world could you afford this?"

The answer? Credit.

There were systems in place for people like me—poor athletes who were gifted but flat broke. When somebody was identified as a player with great potential, those systems were there to welcome that individual with open arms.

I was lucky enough to be one of those players.

Almost out of the blue, I was offered a line of credit to get me through this period and to enable me to train for the draft opportunity. Yes, there were some not-so-great interest rates involved, but I had no other choice. When I got drafted, I would be able to pay the money back and get clear of it.

Not *if* I got drafted—*when* I got drafted.

I didn't know enough to make the best deal. I was still just a kid, really. But I did what I had to do. I knew I had to get ready—and I knew I would use whatever resources were made available to help me get ready.

Going into that training, there were plenty of guys ranked ahead of me that had declared for the draft. As I said, I wasn't seen as a huge prospect—I didn't feel people were really recognizing me. At the same time, I didn't feel like I was taking a long shot going for the draft after my second year of college.

However, many people disagreed with that assessment.

Here are a few actual quotes regarding my chances from some high-level "authorities" at the time, who will remain nameless:

"This whole thing is ludicrous. Let me say the bottom line: One, he's not ready."

"He should stay in school."

"He is making a hell of a mistake."

You'll recall I don't appreciate others judging my abilities—nor do I allow them to have the final word on my future. As a matter of fact, that kind of dismissal fuels my competitive edge. The edge I've carried with me ever since I was a kid and had that horrible experience in the Green Projects.

What was more important to me was the opinion of my previous coach, Quin Snyder. He was the man who, at that time, knew my abilities the best. And he was completely supportive. This is what he told the press:

> *"I believe he's making a decision that suits him well. He's got an outstanding opportunity in front of him. It will be exciting to see him at the next level. Playing in the NBA is something every kid dreams about, but Keyon is one of the few who will have a chance to experience it."*

Once again, I just wanted the opportunity to prove myself. And I did. The workouts with the teams in Atlanta were where I made my ball. All the people that were ranked ahead of me, who were also working out for the same teams?

Well, I just flat-out kicked their butts. It was mano-a-mano, and I was determined to end up as The Man.

Still, in spite of my hard work, in spite of the fact that I outplayed the competition, I was not invited to the actual draft, which was held in Minneapolis, Minnesota, as many other players were.

Not a good harbinger.

But I approached the draft with a positive mindset. I committed to renting a suite at the Marriott Harbor Beach hotel for all my friends and family, so we could celebrate the night of the draft. Most estimates had me ranked at anywhere from 13th down to 35th. But, of course, neither they nor I had any idea what would actually happen.

I just knew this was the day I had worked toward my entire life.

With that in mind, is it any wonder that I was sweating like a madman all day long? I couldn't stop perspiring; heck, I was *smelly*. I would ask people around me if they smelled onions—and then I realized with more than a little embarrassment that the stink was coming from *me*. I put on deodorant like three times that day, but it didn't do me any good. The sweat kept coming; this just didn't happen to me unless I was hooping.

That's how tense I was. But all the blood, sweat, and tears had been worth it. Because, when the draft order was finally announced, I was thrilled beyond words to see where I had landed:

10th.

Yep, Keyon Dooling had made the Top Ten of the NBA draft. I had *just* made it, but there the ESPN commentators were, right on the big-screen TV, saying my name a lot sooner than I had expected. And all of a sudden, all my friends and family that I had invited up to that suite were all around me, giving me one big, giant group hug.

Everybody was screaming with joy—especially me! And then, those emotions flipped, and I was suddenly crying in the arms of my mom and my Pop. I actually had to leave the room to get myself together. It was too intense—my placement in the draft picks was way higher than I had thought possible.

I think it was the first time I ever cried tears of joy. The tears I had cried through the years never had a happy component to them; so this again was something new to me. The whole day was like nothing I had ever experienced or would experience again. My old Dillard high school coach was in the room for the draft announcement to pat me on the back—and my last coach, Quin Snyder, called me to congratulate me.

I was drafted by the Orlando Magic, who immediately traded me, along with Corey Maggette, Derek Strong, and some cash, to the L.A. Clippers that same night. In 2012, one sports columnist named it one of the top five Clipper trades of all time. Now, in 2000, the Clippers were not a strong NBA team; as a matter of fact, they had been the worst team not only in the division, but in the entire NBA! Their hometown rivals, the Lakers, were the ones getting all the titles and the glory.

But going to the Clippers didn't bother me. Nothing could. I was just happy to be *in*. Besides, I knew I was going to be playing ball with my buddy Quentin Richardson, who I had known since I was twelve, when we both played on the Adidas teams. We also had played on the USA basketball team together. We had kept in touch and I was glad I'd have a good friend on the court with me.

WHAT'S DRIVING YOU???

If one picture can tell a story of a thousand words, the picture in the Fort Lauderdale newspaper the next day maybe had a few million more in it. It was a giant color photo of me hugging my dad in the hotel suite after the announcement, with those tears of joy running down my face. That newspaper page is framed and still hangs on the wall of my home today, because it represents one of the truly giant moments of my life.

When I was a kid, we all talked about trying to "make it to the league." It was the ultimate dream. Well, I actually did make it to the league. I made it. Those are always three beautiful words to be able to say—and they were never more beautiful to me than on that particular night.

THE BREAKDOWN:
PART SIX

THE ANNOUNCEMENT

SEPTEMBER 20, 2012.

That was the day the news came out—both from myself and from the Celtics.

This was the statement I authorized my representative to release:

> *"Keyon has decided that he has given the NBA twelve good years and that it's time to pursue other interests and spend more time with his family. He will never forget his time in Boston with the Celtics."*

Danny Ainge put out this statement:

> *"We'll miss Keyon's spirit and energy, both on and off the court. The whole Celtics family wishes him well as he enters the next phase of his life."*

Pursue other interests? Spend more time with his family? Nobody really believed that.

KEYON L. DOOLING

Nobody really believed that I was walking away from an NBA contract with the Boston Celtics for no reason. There was speculation I was angling to get back with the Heat in Miami or the Orlando Magic and get closer to home. Or that I simply thought I didn't have anything left in the tank when it came to playing ball.

Of course, none of that was true. And even though those closest to me couldn't understand why I had quit, I knew I had to do it because of the anxiety I'd been experiencing ever since that night in the men's room. The dream that had fueled most of my life, the dream of being an NBA player, was now something that felt oppressive and draining.

After the announcement, the truth of this hit me in an odd way. When I officially retired and called it quits...

...wow.

I suddenly relaxed for the first time since the incident at the restaurant in Seattle.

The low shot clock was gone. My head was clear. I didn't have any more urges to call people out of the blue to lecture them about Jesus.

The Celtics, backing my transition out of being an active player, had agreed to let me work behind the scenes in their player development division, so I would remain, for the time being, a part of that elite organization.

In short, I felt like I had a pathway to a new future. A difficult couple of weeks—but a happy ending.

Maybe it might have stayed a happy ending, I don't know. I wouldn't get the chance to find out. My sudden retirement was only a Band-Aid on a much bigger wound. And, when the unexpected came flying at me so quickly after that wound was exposed, that Band-Aid was suddenly ripped off before any healing could occur. That, in turn, triggered the final and the most serious part of my breakdown.

All just because I wanted to play with my kids.

SETTING THE TABLE

DANIA BEACH. THAT WAS THE DESIGNATED "Negro" beach I spoke of earlier in this book, the only beach in the Fort Lauderdale area that black people were allowed to go in the old days of segregation—and you could only get there by ferry at the time. It wasn't until 1965 that a road was finally built that allowed vehicles to pass through to the beach area.

Flash forward to the year 2000, my first season in the NBA. Even though I hadn't taken a dime from my parents since the age of sixteen, I still knew I owed them big-time for their support of me through the years. And I was proud that now, thanks to my contract with the Clippers, I was able to buy my mom and dad a condo of their own—right there in Dania Beach.

It had been a long journey—and it didn't just belong to me. After the draft and my trade to the Clippers, it really felt like a *family* goal had been accomplished, which is often the case when a player like me finally reaches the pros. The support of our loved ones can really make the difference between making it and not making it. So I definitely wanted my parents to share in my success.

And my Pop really needed the help. The flower shop was all but done, and he had been working as a skycap at the Fort Lauderdale airport since his recovery from the stroke. Now, finally, he and my mom could get out of the hood and live comfortably. As for me, I was also done struggling to make ends meet.

When you come to the end of a long road, when you've surmounted every challenge along the way to reach a cherished goal, it's a relief. Getting to the NBA was like that for me. It was the end of my amateur status and the beginning of my life as a pro.

When you finally reach a dramatic new stage of your life, however, what you never see coming are the new challenges you must face. In my case, I had three very big surprises all within the same year that would definitely be a harbinger of my thirteen years playing in the NBA.

The first surprise? A very pleasant one.

During the time just before the draft, when I was working out with different NBA teams in Atlanta to show my capabilities, Tosha was there with me. That's when we found out she was with child. It wasn't planned, but I didn't care. I was happy, because I knew this was the woman I wanted to be with and we were going to have a baby together.

However, a lot of people in our families weren't so happy. We were now living together and we weren't married. There was a stigma against "shacking up" in our community—and now, on top of that, we were also going to have a child out of wedlock. So we were criticized.

WHAT'S DRIVING YOU???

But all that conflict simply brought us closer together—as well as closer to Christ. We knew our values and we knew that we would be spending the rest of our lives together.

And, to tell you the truth, I didn't really care what anybody thought because I was a grown man. I had been taking care of myself and my family for years, so basically, my attitude was, "Y'all don't tell me. I'm self-made. Y'all don't tell me. I'm here now." My Pop was cool about it. He treated me like a young man and supported me. But, at the end of the day, it was good to hear everyone else's opinions and understand where they were coming from. It was a teachable moment.

Despite some people's objections, I honestly believe that living together with Tosha before we got married was a good thing. We got to know each other a lot better and sort our relationship out. Every couple has intense battles and power struggles early on, and we were no exception. It's important to know, however, that, with time, you can overcome those conflicts.

A lot of things were magnified because, obviously, when you're a pro NBA player, you're on the road a lot—and my first year with the Clippers made it clear what that meant for both of us. For me, it was a hard mental and physical adjustment—it is an exhausting life, because you need to achieve at as high a level as you can while constantly traveling from one city to the next.

On her end, she was pregnant and she didn't know anybody near our new home, a townhouse in Redondo Beach, an L.A. beach town where we lived during my rookie year. So a lot of the time she was very lonely—and when she wasn't lonely, she was overwhelmed. That's because old Florida friends or family members would frequently show up in California, crash at our place, and turn it into a disaster area! It was my fault—again, everybody wanted to share in my success and also hang out in L.A., so I would give them the green light and forget to tell Tosha about it! That had to stop—so I finally had to tell people not to come out for a while, so she could catch a break.

We came through all of those radical life changes during our first year living together feeling more committed to each other than ever before—and on January 19, 2001, we were blessed with the birth of our first child, our daughter Deneal Catherine. And the following summer, we made our relationship official and got married.

Stigma gone!

The second surprise of my rookie year was *not* so pleasant. I had just gone from having no money to having a whole bunch, thanks to my NBA paychecks. Talk about whiplash! Banking that kind of coin took a lot of pressure off my shoulders, pressure that'd been overwhelming for the past few years. I could take care of my old family—my folks—as well as my new one with Tosha.

So how could having all this cash lead to an *un*pleasant surprise? What I didn't realize or expect was that along with my newfound financial success came a different kind of overwhelming pressure. No, I didn't have to worry about taking care of myself anymore—but suddenly I was made to worry about taking care of everybody else.

I quickly found out that almost everybody I had ever met—people I barely even knew—suddenly wanted a piece of what I had achieved. People wanted to hang around me, people wanted tickets to my games...and a lot of people wanted *money*. Everyone felt a sense of entitlement when it came to my making it to the NBA—even though I was just starting my pro career!

To be honest, I didn't even know how long it would last. The average NBA player's career spans about five years and, since this was my rookie year, I hadn't even really been tested at the pro level yet. Not only that, but, as I would learn from personal experience during my second NBA season, the wrong injury can threaten to end your career at any time.

At that point, I wasn't really worried about my future, I was just catching up with where I had arrived. You have to understand that I was only twenty when I played my first season with the Clippers—and I was, of course, mostly focused on basketball. Everything happened very fast for me; I wasn't very sophisticated about people and I honestly didn't believe certain people would actually try to take advantage of me in the ways they did. I just knew that everyone wanted to share in the dream—and in the beginning, I did everything I could to help out.

My story isn't unusual in that regard. Many other players shared similar experiences with me and I came to discover that a lot of my teammates, especially those who were also from disadvantaged areas, had the same kind of demands placed on them. Those demands led to a constant internal conflict; if you say no too often, you're a bad guy who forgot where he came from, but if you say yes too often, you're viewed as a sucker who's nothing more than an ATM machine.

My relations with people were suddenly upside down. I found myself living in a whole different world that I was definitely not prepared for in any way, shape, or form. There was no blueprint or plan in place for how to deal with that world.

For one thing, I had to spend an incredible amount of time and energy just on being *nice*.

That sounds strange, I know. I have a big heart and I never want to let people down. But when you're trying to focus on training or mentally preparing for a game—or when you're just trying to relax from a rigorous road trip—it can be extremely draining to deal with a constant stream of people wanting things from you.

First, you have to find out what they want. Maybe they just want to meet up with you again or get a picture with you. Simple enough. Maybe they want tickets. Okay, I can try. But maybe…they want to tell you their problems.

That's when it gets tricky.

Things people might have been holding back from their friends and relatives, the very worst problems they had but were too ashamed to tell anybody else? Those were the very things many of them were anxious to unload on me—because I was expected to solve those problems for them.

Don't get me wrong, I know what it's like to not have money and to desperately need it. But it wasn't always a case of need. People being people, some of them were less than honest about things.

It takes a toll on your emotions to try and figure out who's gaming you and who is in genuine need. Through the years, I would end up getting repeatedly shocked and rocked by the bad behavior of some folks I had known from before I made it to the NBA. It's only been recently that I've been able to look back and see clearly what certain people were up to—because I had learned the hard way, through experience, how to judge these situations and to finally set up proper boundaries.

At the time, though, I didn't want to see it, nor did I really understand it.

But you feel it in your soul. You feel lonely, like nobody likes you for yourself, but just for what you can do for them. It was what I felt in college, when everybody was nice to me because I was a star basketball player, but they didn't really care about who I was as a person.

That feeling was amplified a million times during my pro career. It was difficult to say no, even when I knew I should. This might seem like a good problem to have—making so much money that others want some of it—but it affects your relationships with those nearest and dearest to you and it leaves you feeling isolated and alone.

In the end, it would also contribute to my breakdown.

My third and final surprise of my rookie year came when I started playing with the Clippers. It was a good one—*and* it was a bad one at the same time.

The surprise was this: Even though I was a rookie, I was quickly perceived as one of the team *leaders*. I love being a leader, so that was great. What wasn't so great was…I had yet to play an NBA game, and people were looking to me to lead on the pro court?

How did that happen? I'm still not sure—but starting out in that leadership position ended up being an omen of what was to come during my years in the NBA.

QUICK FIRST STEP

AS I ALREADY NOTED, the Clippers were coming off the worst record in the NBA the season before I joined the team. Obviously, seeing that they had to shake things up, they made the big trade that brought me and Corey Maggette to the team on the night I was drafted by the Orlando Magic.

They had one great already playing for them. Lamar Odom had played his rookie season with the team, and made the 2000 NBA All-Rookie First Team. Naturally, he was seen as a key to future success.

Now, in addition to Corey and me, two other highly touted rookie players had been drafted directly by the Clippers to further strengthen the team. As I already mentioned, my old buddy Quentin Richardson was one of them. The other was Darius Miles, drafted right out of high school by the Clippers as the third overall pick, at the time, the highest a player had been drafted directly from high school.

A lot of new talent—accent on the word "new."

The players that management was now counting on to turn things around were all very, very young—nobody over twenty-two (and Darius was only nineteen). It was only Corey and Lamar's second NBA season, and the first for Quentin, Darius, and me. Yet, because we were regarded as the players who were going to "save" the team, the veteran players on the team were following *us* around—maybe because they had had such a bad season the previous year and they were looking to us for the answers. No rap against them, these kinds of weird team dynamics happen.

Only problem with this one? I felt clueless. Yes, *clueless*.

Yeah, I was extremely athletic—and I could run and jump with the best of them. But because I was a young player, I didn't understand the point guard position at the NBA level. I needed teaching. I needed structure. I needed to *learn*.

There was no doubt our young group had a lot of talent. But there was also no doubt that we all needed some serious seasoning as pro players. I had no idea how much I *didn't* know about NBA play until I joined the Miami Heat a few years later.

So, yeah, we were leaders. Leaders who didn't know anything!

I was even seen as a leader within our little group of newbies. That's because I was the one who already had a family, and I wanted to share my blessings and my home with my new teammates. Tosha and me would organize and host what I called "Sunday Dinners," even though they might just as easily happen on a Tuesday or Wednesday.

Most often, Quentin and Darius would join us for these cookouts and potluck dinners—I was the tightest with those two. I had known Quentin since I was twelve—and Darius had also known Quentin since he was twelve—so Q brought us together, by telling each of us how great the other was!

Our Sunday Dinners continued the whole time we were playing for the Clippers. Everybody needed to come and bring their dishes—and a lot of the older players would come and join in our little impromptu feasts. Sometimes, when their relatives were in town, the players' parents and even their grandparents would come along—we'd have three or four generations of family at the table.

Awesome times.

My team may have seen me as a leader way before they should've—but the real NBA elites on other clubs quickly let me know what my status *really* was. Defensive great Gary Payton, playing in his prime as a point guard for the Seattle SuperSonics, took aim at me in my very first preseason NBA game. Right when I checked in, he looked at my coach, Alvin Gentry, and said, "Alvin! I know you're not gonna put this little young, dumb, punk motherf—er on me!"

I was confused. So confused that the only thing I could contribute to the conversation was "Huh?"

That just invited more trouble.

"What did you say?" Gary asked me, glaring at me.

"I didn't really say anything," was my next witty remark.

"You talkin' s—? I'm gonna bust your little ass."

"No, I'm not doin' anything!"

And that's how it went, every time we played Seattle. For my first two seasons, every time I saw Gary Payton, he trash-talked me! I came to find out he did that to all the guards when they came on game day, just to see if they could deal with the challenge. My third season, I had apparently passed his little test. He said, "All right, I see you've got heart," and from that moment on, he didn't do me like that anymore.

But incidents like that made me anxious to prove myself against players at that level. Six games into my rookie season, I got the opportunity—and maybe got a little carried away in the process.

Dikembe Mutombo had already won three Defensive Player of the Year awards and was on his way to his fourth when I went up against him and the Atlanta Hawks that season. He would end up holding second place in the number of blocked shots in the history of the NBA. Needless to say, he was feared on the court. He was also famous for wagging his finger and shaking his head at any player who he had stopped from scoring.

During this particular game, I was flying down the lane with the ball—and I saw Mutombo waiting for me at the rim. Well, this was one shot that didn't get blocked—lil ol' six foot, five inches me flew up over seven foot, two inches Mutombo, and I dunked on him.

Then I broke out his finger wag on *him*.

Yeah, I got a technical foul called for doing that—my first tech in the NBA—but I was way too excited at having pulled that off to stop myself. Besides, I had seen my idol, Michael Jordan, do it, so I just wanted to emulate the best. You can still find video of that dunk on YouTube, by the way.

The biggest game of the season for me personally didn't have much to do with the score. It was a night when I set a new Clippers record, even though it had nothing to do with what I did on court.

It was when we came to Miami for the first time to play the Heat—my first NBA game back in South Florida. It was February 14, Valentine's Day, and I got all the love I could imagine. And that record?

It was for acquiring the most tickets for a road game.

Between my dad and me, we came up with 168 of them for family and friends. Pop did most of the heavy lifting, getting 125 of those tickets and spreading them out throughout the old neighborhood.

Fortunately, I played well that night with a couple of highlight plays and I finished with six points in fourteen minutes. The bad part was that we ended up losing in OT, 101-99. Still, that was a pretty good result against the far superior Heat team of veterans under the outstanding coaching skills of the legendary Pat Riley.

More than 160 people from my past came to see me play. High school classmates, church groups, relatives, friends…almost everybody was there, including all of my past coaches from my youth. Judge Zebedee Wright, from my youth traveling team, was watching with my dad, as was my Dillard Coach, Darryl Burrows, and Mark Wilson from Cardinal Gibbons.

Coach Wilson was kind enough to tell the *Sun Sentinel*, "I'm not surprised (Keyon) got to this level. He has all the tools and he has the demeanor. On top of it all, he is everything people say he is. He is a nice young man and you like to see nice people be successful."

Can't get much nicer than that, Coach Wilson.

The Clippers did improve in the 2000-2001 season—from a 15-67 record the previous year to a 31-51 record. We were no longer the worst, but we were still a long way from first. As for myself, during my rookie year, I felt I played some good basketball. My athleticism had helped me compensate for my lack of NBA experience.

But even that would be taken away from me in the next season.

INJURY

IT WAS ONLY EIGHT GAMES into my sophomore season that my ankle gave out on me.

November 14, 2001. We were playing the Bulls and a collision put me down on the court. An impact injury. The papers called it a sprained left ankle.

The truth was nobody knew what was wrong.

I couldn't put any weight on it and the doctors couldn't figure out what was causing the pain. Me, I was twenty-two years old and scared—I had never been hurt like that before. Yeah, I had another year on my contract—but after that?

At first, they said I would be out for six weeks. After those six weeks were up, I was still unable to play. I told the *Los Angeles Times* in January of 2002, "I'm really frustrated. I want to play. It's hard to even watch the games. I still feel a part of the team. I still get into the locker room trash talk."

I tried to practice, but I couldn't run or do jump shots. I could only do standing shots. Toward the end of the season, I did manage to play a few games—but there was no doubt the ankle was an issue, so I didn't get much playing time.

While all this was going on, while I was trying to get back on the court, while I was getting all these different opinions on what was going on with my ankle, my mental toughness was being questioned. People were saying, "Maybe this kid wasn't ready for the NBA, maybe he came out too early for the draft."

And I had to really question whether I had a future as an NBA player. Nobody could properly treat my ankle since nobody could figure out what was wrong; so, I didn't know how serious it was.

That was the injury that changed my whole life. I thought I was going to be a $100 million man, playing basketball with the amount of talent that I had and with my build compared to other guys who had come before me. I thought I had a chance to make my mark in the NBA—now, who knew?

The low shot clock was back in my head and it was definitely ticking as loudly as it ever had.

For the first time, I thought about my long-term future. I took out life insurance and got some other financial ducks in a row. I had to plan beyond the NBA—and, since I wasn't playing much, I had plenty of time to do that. Altogether, I only played in fourteen games during my second season out of our eighty-plus game schedule.

As a side note, for those of you who wonder why people making as much money as I was at the time would ever have to worry about their finances, *Sports Illustrated* reported in 2009 that within five years of retirement, an estimated 60 percent of former NBA players are broke. That's right, within five years. Expenses are heavy during your playing years and if you don't plan accordingly, it's easy to crash and burn once you leave the court for good.

All that weighed heavily on my mind as, that summer, I had surgery on my ankle. They discovered the problems and, thank God, fixed them. Going into my third season as a Clipper, though, I still wasn't 100 percent. I had lost my athletic edge. I went without a dunk for two years and suddenly, I had to refocus my approach to a ground game.

But, as I've said, out of bad always comes good—and the good thing that came out of this difficult period was the fact that I had to improve my mental game; it was the only way to compensate for what I had lost because of my ankle injury. I simply had to learn how to become a better NBA-level point guard. Just like an aging baseball pitcher who's lost some speed has to make up for it by being smarter about what he throws, I had to rely on brains, not brawn. That improved my mental game in the NBA which, in turn, was crucial to my overall development.

That development, however, took time. I ended up learning a lot from Dennis Johnson, who was named head coach about two-thirds of the way through my third season. But, when I came back for my fourth and final season with the Clippers, there was yet another coaching change, one that did not work in my favor.

When you're told, as I was, that you aren't cut out to be an NBA player...well, let's just say that can affect your attitude. This person didn't just let it go at that, he continued to tell me in great detail why I wasn't cut out to be an NBA player.

"You're not a point guard. You're not a shooting guard. You don't dribble well. You don't handle well. You've got some quickness, but I just think it's going to be hard for you to make a living in this league."

Okay, then.

If you've read everything up to this point, you know nothing fuels me more than being told I can't do something. Nothing motivates me more than an authority figure judging my abilities and deciding I'm going to somehow come up short. What was also slightly reassuring was the fact that I knew I wasn't the only player he had said this to.

So my answer to this gentleman was this:

"I don't believe you. I don't think you're the greatest coach either. If you feel that way about me, trade me, waive me, cut me, do something, because this is how I provide for my family and I deserve the opportunity to show what I can do."

Well, despite those words, they didn't trade me. I don't know why, but I was there the whole season. And that turned out to be a good thing for them and for me. When some other players on the team ended up on the bench because of injuries, they had to play me more. It was the chance I asked for, even though the coaching staff didn't particularly want to give it to me. For my part, I was, as usual, determined to show everybody what I could do—so I came back strong to finish my last season with the Clippers on a positive note.

As a matter of fact, during that last part of my final Clippers season, I showed Gary Payton himself how much heart I had developed during the past four years. Gary was now with the Lakers—and, somehow, our team managed to pull out a rare win against him and the rest of our tough-as-nails crosstown rivals. Here's how the *Los Angeles Times* wrote it up:

> *Gary Payton can be excused for not seeing Keyon Dooling.*
>
> *Nobody has seen much of the Clipper guard lately.*
>
> *But given some playing time, though not a starting spot, because of an injury to Marko Jaric, Dooling has responded spectacularly. Sunday night at Staples Center, he soared from behind with 3.9 seconds remaining to block a layup attempt by the Lakers' Payton that could have tied the score in a game the Clippers won, 101-98.*

That was the closing of the circle. When the season was over, the Clippers were done with me and I was done with them. It had been a difficult start to my NBA career. The team, overall, was too young and underwent too many coaching changes during my time there. And my ankle injury during my second year ended up blocking any momentum I might have built.

But, as always, the good comes with the bad; there were beautiful parts to the Clipper experience. We fell in love with California; we forged some relationships and some friendships out there that are stronger now than ever. Tosha and I began our family there and had another daughter, Gabrielle Latrail, in September of my final season in 2003.

Bigger family, bigger responsibilities. But now I was a free agent. Even though I had finished strong with the Clippers, my overall limited playing time that last season had hindered my future NBA options. People weren't exactly beating down the doors to sign me up.

Once again, I had to prove myself.

More importantly, I needed to understand what real leadership was all about. And back home in South Florida, I was about to do just that.

THE BREAKDOWN:
PART SEVEN

THE ARREST

THE STORM HAD PASSED.

I felt like I finally had made a new beginning. The first day after I retired I got a job offer from the front office of an NBA team. I also had some other business ventures that I was working on and they looked really promising.

There could be a life after the NBA. And it could be a great life.

I *felt* great. My body had been really, really hurting because of all my past injuries and what I had put it through during my twelve-year NBA career—not to mention the recent pain and depression I had been going through. Now, again, I thought I was moving past that giant dark cloud. I had been focusing so hard on my game since I was five years old—this was the first time in more than twenty-five years that that pressure was gone.

I almost felt like a kid again.

Of course, the friends and family members who had been watching the events of the last week or so weren't so sure that I was as all right as I said I was. They watched in shock as I abruptly retired from what they considered THE dream career. My decision seemed to come out of no-where—and none of my explanations for making it seemed to make sense.

Even my own wife didn't know what to make of me. Yes, we had talked and talked and talked about what I was going through, but I still hadn't shared what had happened to me as a child with anyone, including her, so Tosha just couldn't understand why I had gone as crazy as I had in Seattle or why I felt I had to quit basketball.

She just knew she had to keep praying for me and keep being there for her husband—so she did.

It had only been a couple days since I had officially retired. We were still in the house we had rented for the season in Wellesley, a nice neighborhood just outside of Boston. I woke up that morning wanting to have some fun with my kids. They, of course, knew something big had happened to me—that something had been seriously wrong with daddy. I wanted to reassure them and do a relaxing activity to reestablish our family bonds.

I was overdue to give them some quality dad time.

Now, if you happen to search the Dooling Family on YouTube, you'll find a video we did a few months before all this happened. The video was called "Sportsality," and it shows us doing a fun workout with our kids. That's the kind of thing I had in mind that morning—and that's all. Blow off some steam, spend some quality time with the kids, and enjoy ourselves as a family.

We went out into the street in front of our home. I was excited, happy, showing the kids how to slap box. We were also dancing and, again, just having a good time. It was a little cloudy and cool, so I remember trying to move into the sun where we would all be warmer.

I can't really explain what happened next, because I don't know *why* it happened.

Apparently, one of the neighbors thought we shouldn't be playing in the street and that we were playing a little too rough. Me and the kids did roughhouse a little, but it was never anything serious. I'm a physical guy and it was just the way we played. Nobody ever got hurt, that intention was definitely never a part of what we did. It was only about fun.

Anyway, soon after we went back into the house, I heard a knock at the door. It was a little before noon and this was a *big* knock: BOOM BOOM BOOM! And I thought, "Who's this knocking on the door like they're the police?"

I didn't know how right I was.

"This is the police, open the door!" came a voice from the other side.

What???

Suddenly, my short-lived euphoria went up in smoke. Everything became a blur—and the low shot clock came back with a vengeance. I was breathing hard, I was scared, angry, and feeling very paranoid.

And that is never the state you want to be in when you greet the police.

I opened the door and saw I had a reason to be paranoid. There were cops *everywhere*. Cops over here, cops over there, squad cars all over the street with their lights on, and the cops were yelling at me, "Get on the ground! Get on the ground! Get on the ground!"

Keep in mind that I was standing inside my own home, not doing one damned thing. I didn't know who called the police on me or why. I didn't know if this was a racial thing or not. I only knew that there were way too many cops threatening me for…what?

I got on the ground and they actually cuffed me. My wife and kids watched all this go down and were crying. They didn't know what was going on—and I was becoming more and more unhinged. I was cracking—I almost blacked out. I suddenly felt like I didn't know who I was anymore.

The cops, meanwhile, went through the house and "investigated" to make sure the kids were okay. They were, of course. Me, I was the only one who was deeply injured. I was in a paranoid-schizophrenic state and this was the first time I had ever been in handcuffs—and this was happening in front of my children!

Again, I could not process this, because my mental state was even more fragile than I had guessed. I just kept telling the cops, "I don't know what's going on with me, just take me to the hospital so they can find out what's wrong with me."

In the end, the cops were cool. They didn't arrest me; they even took the cuffs off me. They saw I was in a bad state and they drove me to the hospital as I had asked. They were bending over backward to be nice because they felt incredibly guilty—they could see for themselves that we were a nice family in a nice house and they had been called on a wild goose chase by an overzealous neighbor. When I look back on this incident, I see clearly that it wasn't their fault—it happened because of whoever called them.

WHAT'S DRIVING YOU???

I never found out who that neighbor was or what he or she was thinking—but the aftermath of that thoughtless call was brutal. Suddenly, I was in a hospital under observation. They could see how agitated I was, but they didn't have a room for me—so they transferred me to a psychiatric hospital that was supposedly one of the best in the country.

I had asked to be hospitalized. I had made this happen. Now...I had to deal with the bottom floor.

COACHING

THE NEWS WAS AS BIG as it gets in the NBA: Shaquille O'Neal was coming to Miami, after demanding to be traded from the division-winning L.A. Lakers.

Another piece of news wasn't *quite* so big: Keyon Dooling was also coming to Miami, after not being picked up by the division-*losing* L.A. Clippers.

Maybe my news didn't make headlines, but the impact of the Heat on my life would end up being huge.

As I told my hometown paper, "It's a fresh start for me and my family, and most importantly I get Shaquille O'Neal on top of that." Best of all, my family and I could live in our home in the Fort Lauderdale area—and all of my friends and family members could come see me play bball on a regular basis.

It felt good. It felt right. And it turned out to be amazing.

After the Clippers let me go, I had to scramble to get signed by another team. I was offered a minimum deal by the Miami Heat—that meant I would be taking a pay cut of more than half of what I was making in L.A.

KEYON L. DOOLING

But it was more than worth the pay cut. Basketball legend Pat Riley had put together an amazing organization in Miami that's still a steamroller today. That organization was about to completely transform my mindset and my skills in a way I had never expected—and provide me with two of the most important mentors I would have during my NBA years. One of those mentors would change my life on the court—the other would change it *off* the court.

Let's talk about the first of my two pivotal mentors at the Heat, Coach Stan Van Gundy. Coach Van Gundy had already been with the Heat for eight years when I arrived. He had been assistant coaching under Pat Riley for the first few years and then got bumped up to head coach the season before, as Riley had decided to focus on the executive side of running the team.

So Riley had personally trained my new coach to help players excel in every way possible—which probably explains why Coach Van Gundy pushed me in a way I had never been pushed by a coach.

That pushing began with our first training sessions—when I questioned for the first time whether I actually wanted to continue to play pro basketball! That's because the intensity of the player training program in Miami was incredible. It was my fifth year as a pro, I was twenty-four years old, and I was suddenly getting challenged like I never had been before.

We began by running on the track at the University of Miami. The first day we got there, we had to run six 800s (each 800 was about half a mile), and you had to do each 800 within a time limit in order to move on to the next phase of training.

184

WHAT'S DRIVING YOU???

Well, I got to the fourth 800 and, even though my times were good, I was starting to cave because of the heat and humidity in South Florida, especially at that time of year. I was sweating like there was no tomorrow—and I really wasn't sure if I could keep going.

The other guys? They were looking good, because they were used to this level of training, but I sure wasn't. I was shocked that they worked us this hard this fast. But soon, I came to realize this was how things should be done.

As training progressed, Coach Van Gundy was hard on me, very hard. He wanted me to learn what I needed to do on the court. He made me prove myself, and once I got what he was trying to teach me, he let up. It was a winning combination of old school/new school coaching techniques.

The new school part came in the way I felt able to feel free to communicate with him—even at full blast! I can be a very emotional player, and sometimes, I would confront him with an outburst of anger or frustration. Well, he never would take that personally. As a matter of fact, he'd get right up there at my level, and yell right back at me! I didn't mind that kind of intense talkback, because it was honest and let me know exactly what he was after from me.

As a matter of fact, he taught me how not to take things personally. "It's not personal! Do your job!" was his mantra. When I wasn't feeling it, he would pull me into his office and say, "Keyon, hey listen, you're not positive today. I know it's not going the way you like, it's probably not fair but that's what it is right now. I know you can deal with all that, because you're a positive person—that's who you are. I see your family around here, I know your story. I know where

185

you're from. You come from a hardworking background. You keep working and you will crack the rotation. Just do your job and it will show."

I did just that—and it did show. It was an unbelievable experience. And, from then on, I took that philosophy with me to other teams.

As a matter of fact, I took everything with me that I learned there. I learned different systems, different views, different perceptions of the game, and developed a different appreciation of the game. I fell in love with basketball all over again. I was only at the Heat for one season, but I got a lifetime's worth of discipline, focus, knowledge, and understanding.

What specifically did Coach Van Gundy do for me? He finally helped me define myself as an NBA player.

My coach from Cardinal Gibbons had told the press near the end of my tenure at the Clippers, "Keyon's problems have had to do with the Clippers' indecisiveness…If he gets to the right system and they let him know exactly what they want him to be, he could be in this league for ten years." Coach Wilson didn't know how true his words would become.

Coming to the pros, the big knock against me was that I was a "tweener." That meant I wasn't quite a point guard and I wasn't quite a shooting guard. I could do both, but wasn't accomplished enough at either of them to own them. And I never had the opportunity to learn enough to really change that perception.

Under Coach Van Gundy's guidance, I began to evolve to a combo player, the opposite of a tweener. When you're a combo player, that means you can indeed own both guard positions. Because of what I was taught at the Heat, I finally was given the right foundation to build from as a player. I found out I could do a lot more on the court, and that, in turn, increased my value as an NBA player.

Van Gundy's coaching staff was almost as awesome as he was. Current world champion Heat coach, Erik Spoelstra, was his assistant coach; I used to watch game video with him and he taught me another level of the game from that. Former NBA players Keith Askins and Bimbo Coles also served as coaches and helped my development immensely. They were tough on me at the start as well, until they saw I was going to be a good soldier and deliver what they wanted.

And of course, there were great players on the Heat that also poured their wisdom into me. Players like the all-time great Shaq, the legendary Dwyane Wade (still playing with the Heat as I write these words) who was just becoming a superstar, Steve Smith (who's now with NBA TV), and Damon Jones, who was one of the funniest, loudest characters I ever met. They all contributed to my rebirth in the NBA.

As did one other player, who would prove to be my *other* important mentor at the Heat.

I believe that if I had played with Eddie Jones my first year in the NBA, I would have become a better player and had a more successful career. Eddie, like me, was from Broward County in Florida, from Pompano Beach to be exact. He was a few years older than me and played for one of Dillard High's rival schools. I remember watching him play against Dillard when I was a young kid—everybody knew Eddie was real good back then. We had talked a few times when I had played for the Clippers, but never spent any significant time together until we became teammates on the Heat.

This guy was unbelievable.

You've probably seen those Dos Equis beer ads featuring "The Most Interesting Man in the World?" Well, that was who Eddie was for real to me. I'd say, "Eddie, what's in your cup?", and he'd shoot back, "Oh, hey man, this is a Lowland Scotch, Johnnie Walker Blue." I expected him to add "Shaken, not stirred," because although he wasn't 007, he was pretty darned close.

In a lot of ways, I was still basically a kid from the hood at that time—so Eddie took it upon himself to school me on how an NBA player should act *off* the court. For example, he would show me how to properly dress for different occasions, where to go in certain cities, how to order in a nice restaurant, and just basically how to live a sophisticated life. He'd say, "Hey, this is a sponsor event, you wear this type of attire." Or, "Hey, we're going to New York and going to this steakhouse. They have good food; this is where you go and this is what wine you order." Or, "If you're coming to a game, get to the arena early and get your shots up before practice."

I learned how to interact with other people and cultures I had never gotten the chance to know, and how to move in higher circles with more ease and sophistication. These were the things my mom and dad didn't know because they had never gotten the chance to learn them for themselves—but they're critically important if you want to connect with influential people and come across as a substantial person.

That's why, when you find someone who is willing to

help you expand your knowledge in these areas, you should hang on and not let go. I didn't. All season long, he was a coach of a different kind—a life coach.

I rode on private planes for the first time with Eddie. We went to the fights together. He showed me how to have a great, quality vacation when he took me and my family to the Bahamas. You have to understand, I didn't really know what a vacation could be or should be. I didn't really know how enjoyable it was just to sit out by a pool at a resort for an afternoon until Eddie showed me how to do it!

What Eddie did for me was a big turning point—because, from then on, I wanted to do for other younger players what he did for me. Many of them, like me, came from very humble beginnings and didn't know what to do when they were suddenly making millions and expected to act a certain way in social situations. That's why you see so many pro athletes get into trouble; they feel confused and lost, but have to act that macho part, so they don't admit it. They never learn how to handle their new lives or handle themselves in the pros. Many get lost and confused, simply because no one is there to show them the way.

That's why, after I left the Heat, I wanted to mentor others. Obviously, I mentored them in my own way as Eddie and I are different people. But I wanted to emulate his generosity of spirit and once again, be a leader. But this time I would be an all-around leader, not just on the court—that was my goal. Eddie empowered me to go on to do that. He taught me so much.

But there was one more person at the Heat who would teach me the most important lessons of all.

PAT RILEY

I WAS RAISED BY MY POP to be a leader. On almost all of my teams growing up, I was the "hype man," the guy who pumped up the team before a game to motivate them. Now, sometimes that didn't work out so good, like when I was twelve and decided to throw some extreme trash talk at the travel team from Miami we were playing that day. That had a boomerang effect; it pumped *them* up to the point where they came out ready to kill us, and they did—at least on the scoreboard!

That taught me a huge lesson. From then on, I always tried to step up and lead not by being obnoxious and big-mouthed, but by leading from within—by being the example of what to do rather than *telling* everybody what to do. If I lived my values, if I walked the walk, I felt that others would walk with me. I would always be a hype man—but I did it without negativity.

Leadership was always something I tried to bring to any team I played on. In the NBA, however, even though I was initially looked at as a leader, I didn't have the leadership knowledge or skills to *be* that leader. I didn't really *know* how to make the most of my life as a pro athlete on and off the court. I was a very young guy who desperately wanted that knowledge and those skills, but didn't know where to get them.

Yes, my father had told me to be a leader. But he had also told me, "In order to be a good leader, you've got to be a good follower—so you've got to follow the right people until you're ready to lead."

Thanks to Pat Riley, I had finally met the right people. And he was the one who had brought us together.

Those of you who are basketball fans already know plenty about Pat Riley, but, for those of you who aren't, here are a few of his career accomplishments:

- Head coach of five NBA championship teams
- Head coach of the NBA All-Star Game team nine times
- Named one of the ten greatest coaches in NBA history
- The first and *only* North American sports figure to win a championship as a player, assistant coach, head coach, and team executive

His commitment to excellence is well-known—and well-deserved. And, even though I had limited time with him, that time proved crucial to my life evolution.

As I said earlier in this chapter, the Heat coaching staff had to work hard to bring me up to their level of play. That meant I didn't get to play a lot once the season started.

Me being me, I wanted more playing time. As usual, I

was driven by a need to show the team what I could do. Adding to that motivation was the fact that I was playing NBA games in Miami, twenty-five minutes away from my parents' home. My folks would come to every single home game that year—and, of course, a lot of other friends and family members would come as well.

And there I was, sitting on the bench. And, obvious to all, not so happy.

Yeah, I had become a good soldier, but I was hungry for playing time. As a matter of fact, I was mad. I didn't want my time at the Heat to be like my time at the Clippers; I was a pro and I wanted to show it and I wasn't getting the opportunity early on in the season.

So when I got the call to go see Pat Riley in his office, I didn't know what was up. I was like, "Oh, Pat wants to see me? S–t."

Maybe I was in trouble because I was visibly frustrated about all the bench warming I was having to do. Or maybe I was in trouble for something else. After all, it was a strict program in Miami in every regard. For example, you had your weight taken and your body fat measured on a regular basis, and, if those two things weren't right, they could fine you for it. Me, I was a skinny guy and I could lose weight very quickly during the season—I might be below where I should be.

Whatever was going on, I felt like I was going into the principal's office. And the principal, in this case, was one of the most legendary names in the NBA. *Of all time.*

I sat down and quickly found out I wasn't in trouble. Nothing like that. But he *had* noticed my frustration and anger. The meeting wasn't about lecturing me, however; it was about helping me.

"Don't get frustrated," he told me. "Look, you should be mad; you should be pissed off. But what are you going to do with that anger? You've got to *channel it.*"

I told him that I felt like I had a lot of talent and I could help the team if I got some playing time. He told me what to do. He said, "Well, what you've got to do is find out what the coach wants from you. You've got to watch game films and you've got to look at yourself to see what you're doing wrong and what you're doing right."

He went on to relate his philosophy in terms I could apply in a practical way. He told me he liked to get players when they were at peak performance and train them with military precision—and then explained to me how he viewed competition and basketball, in a way that felt like it was right out of *The Art of War* or something.

"Don't let anybody see you complain about not playing," he went on to tell me. "Don't let anybody see you frustrated. Let them see you in the gym. Let them see you in the film room. Let them see you in practice. Let them see you being a professional. Let them see you when you're on the bench; don't sit at the end, sit by the coach so you can hear what he's saying and you can know what's going on in the game. Let them see you cheering; you're a naturally positive person. *Use that.*"

Then he went an extra step with me. I don't know if he saw leadership potential in me, because I certainly didn't believe I was displaying much of it at the time. But he gave me a book, *The 21 Irrefutable Laws of Leadership*

WHAT'S DRIVING YOU???

by John C. Maxwell, and suggested I read it.

I'm still reading books by that author to this day.

The wisdom I obtained from Pat Riley and the book he gave me helped me unlock the leadership skills I wanted and needed. Just as I now had a foundation from which to build my basketball skills from, I also had a foundation from which to build my leadership skills.

But I wasn't ready to lead yet. For the rest of that season, I followed, just as my Pop told me to. I totally gave myself to this team I loved. I stopped caring about how many minutes I played. I was playing with Shaq, I was playing with Wade, I was playing with Eddie Jones, I was playing for the Heat, and I was doing it all right down the I-95 from my old hometown. That was more than good enough for me.

I surrendered completely and gave it all up to the team. I did what Pat Riley told me and I just kept getting better and better as he said I would. I finally cracked the rotation.

And I finally cracked the secrets to succeeding in the NBA.

It kept getting better. We finished first in our division, and for the first time, I was on a postseason team. It was a big contrast from the year before. The year after my final season with the Clippers was done, the closest I got to the playoffs was going to the American Airlines Arena and watching all seven postseason games that the Heat played in Miami.

This year, I didn't have to watch from the stands—I was on the Heat and I was on the court.

And suddenly, I realized I was really becoming an NBA veteran. I had already played in 275 NBA games during my first five seasons—and only six players in that year's playoffs had played in more games than me.

195

KEYON L. DOOLING

What was the experience of my first playoffs like? Unbelievable. It's hard to explain. As intense as the regular season was, as tough and rigorous as the training had been from the start, all of it got turned up a few more notches. The days were longer, there were a lot more team meetings, and we had to watch every piece of film we could get on the opposition. Turned out we were supposed to know everything about every player we would be going up against, up to and including what kind of gum they chewed.

To pump us up, Shaq, Eddie, and the other veterans did more team-building activities for us younger players. One great moment was when Shaq broke out all his NBA championship rings—and said we could each have a ring of our own if we played hard enough in the upcoming series.

We did play hard. The level of basketball was the highest I had ever experienced up until that point. It was like the difference between high school ball and college ball, or the difference between regular season college ball and NCAA tournament ball. Only this was the peak of the mountain. This was the NBA playoffs.

Shaq kept telling us all it would take was sixteen wins to be the NBA champs. We didn't get those sixteen, but we came close. We were eliminated during the Eastern Conference Finals by Detroit, but we didn't make it easy for the Pistons; we took them all the way to seven games. And, man, it was great to go that far.

The next year, Miami would go all the way. The Heat would take the NBA championship. But I wouldn't be there to celebrate.

To be honest, I didn't feel like I could afford to be there.

DRIVE

AS I SAID, I HAD A MINIMUM DEAL during my year with the Heat. But, after I had demonstrated my value there, I was suddenly offered the biggest contract of my life from another team. Even though I loved playing for the Heat, again, I had to think long-term and remember that I had only so many years to play in the NBA.

I had to go for the big contract.

And ironically, the team that offered me that contract was the one that had originally drafted me and immediately traded me to the Clippers. Yep, I was going to the Orlando Magic. I would still be in my home state, just a few hundred miles away from home.

I had taken away a lot from my experience with the Heat. I had finally mastered my NBA guard positions, thanks to my intensive and intelligent training in Miami. I was brought in as a backup for both shooting guards and point guards. I became that combo man that was prized in the league—which is why I was offered such a great deal.

I also now knew what leadership was all about, thanks to Pat Riley, and I intended to make the most of it. Not only that, but my leadership was suddenly valued. Most of the team in Orlando was younger than me, so I was seen as a skilled, seasoned veteran. When I arrived, I was elected team captain.

I was also anxious to expand my influence and my network beyond whatever team I happened to be playing for. That's why I asked to be named player rep to the NBA players' union, the National Basketball Players Association (NBPA). It was an easy request to grant—nobody else wanted to do it!

Getting involved with the union was another facet of my new long-term thinking. After my playing days were over, I knew I wanted to continue to be around the game. What I didn't know was, could a brother get in? What would my role be? Where would I fit in? Where *could* I fit in?

Coaching seemed an obvious path, but I wasn't so sure that it should be my path. Then I expanded my vision; I began to recognize that some ex-players had become GMs of teams, some had careers in broadcasting and politics, and some, like Magic Johnson or Junior Bridgeman, just did fantastic things in the business world.

There truly were great opportunities out there that I had to explore—and it was time to begin that journey. I was in my fifth season—and five years was the average length of an NBA player's career, so, once again, that low shot clock was ticking and I felt like I needed to take action. My role as union rep was the first step toward going beyond the court—and the first time I really got a behind-the-scenes peek at the business of the game.

To be honest, just a year earlier, I was pretty much blind to what the union was all about. Once again, it had been up to the Heat to school me—and they most definitely did.

Guys like Christian Laettner, as well as Eddie Jones and Shaq, had been big on the NBPA. A new negotiation was about to come up, so Shaq and the other vets would tell us young guys, "It's going to be your league! How can you not know what's going on? If you don't care about your business, you're going to get taken advantage of!" I was made to understand what the union did for us and I came to realize how important that organization was to all our futures.

When I got to Orlando, I felt like I needed to do for my new teammates what the Heat players had done for me; educate them and properly represent them. Also, I wanted to expand my own horizons. So I stepped out in front and said, "Hey, I want to be the rep. I need to be the rep because I'm definitely going to go to the meetings to see what's going on—and y'all might not."

And I did. I went to the regular meetings in Vegas, L.A., or wherever they were held, as well as the summer meetings in the Bahamas (not a bad assignment, I gotta say). I met the all top guys at the NBPA, including Billy Hunter, who was then the executive director and would later reach out his hand during my breakdown.

At first, I followed, as I did at the Heat. I was the quiet guy in the room. I still didn't know much, so I just wanted to go and soak up how things worked before I opened my mouth.

What I learned was pretty eye-opening.

It was kind of like being on a never-ending episode of *Game of Thrones*. On the players' side, it was our livelihood; losing on a point could cost us $100 million collectively. On the owners' side, that was $100 million out of their pockets if we won. Not many play this level of a high-stakes game.

Everybody was there to make money and everybody there wanted to see the game continue to grow. But everybody had different ideas of how to make those things happen and who should get what. And sometimes you never knew who to trust. There would actually be moles spying on our side that we didn't find out about until much later.

As I said, I sat back and took it all in. For the first two years as the team rep, I watched all the older guys talk things out, while I soaked up what was happening and why it was going that way.

I was networking at the meetings as well; I had a few years in the league so I knew a lot of different people. I, in turn, was known and respected. Luckily, networking is something I have a natural gift for, a gift that was developed by working for my dad's business when I was a kid.

The secret behind my networking? Simple. I always spoke to everybody.

That might sound obvious, but some NBA players, they might walk by each other and never say a word. Not me. Other players know I'm going to speak to them. They also know, because I'm a fan of the game, I will say something specific about them that will begin a conversation and give us something to continue to talk about when I see them again.

WHAT'S DRIVING YOU???

Two years in, some of the older players, guys like my old friend Dikembe Mutombo, began to retire from the board—and spots became available for the union's executive committee. We were asked if we wanted to go for the higher offices—and, frankly, I didn't. Because I wasn't an NBA superstar, I didn't feel I had enough clout in the league to do the union good in a higher office.

Guys were raising their hands and I didn't. However, Etan Thomas, then playing for the Washington Wizards, raised my hand for me. He went ahead and nominated me for a VP position and I was chosen to serve in that role.

I was twenty-six and now the youngest guy on the executive committee. I had gone from not really knowing much about the union two and a half years before, to playing a part in negotiating what would be potentially the biggest collective bargaining agreement (CBA) in the history of the NBA—or anywhere else for that matter.

And now, instead of watching how the union did its business, I began to observe how the NBA did its business by listening to David Stern, who was the commissioner of the NBA for three decades, as well as the team owners. I was interacting with a group of billionaires over the course of at least fifty meetings that I attended—and if you didn't think I was going to latch on to some of the knowledge they had to offer, you don't know much about me!

At the same time, I obviously needed to represent the players as strongly as I could. We had a position to protect and I wanted to be there for the players and fight for what's right. And I always made it a point to communicate as clearly as possible what was going on to my Magic teammates. I wanted to empower them in the same way the Heat empowered me. For example, the union also had a lot of resources available to players that I was never aware of until I served on the board. I wanted my guys to know about everything they could get out of the NBPA beyond contract negotiations.

I had to learn a lot myself, however. I had to understand our CBA inside and out, since that was the contract we played under, and I also had to handle the inevitable politics of dealing both with other union members as well as the NBA side. I saw how people negotiated long-term, by asking for certain things in exchange for certain other things, in order to move closer to their ultimate goals.

This was heady stuff for a guy whose only executive experience was helping run his dad's flower shop as a boy.

I have to say it was amazing to see the NBA machine in action, because it was an incredibly well-oiled and powerful machine. It was also intimidating to see that, in the end, it was a machine you couldn't really stop. Still, we needed to push back to protect our players, because the NBA will always go after the biggest advantage it can get. That's only natural; within any business system, you're always going to have that dynamic.

At the same time, I could see that I could find a place for myself around the NBA after my playing days were done. Although we might be opponents at the negotiating table, I could still connect with them on a human level when we left the table. And I took away a lot from dealing with these people.

WHAT'S DRIVING YOU???

Two years after being elected to a VP role, I was elected first vice president—which meant I was second only to the president and I ran the meetings when he was unable to attend. It also meant that I would be on the front lines when the NBA lockout hit in 2012.

That lockout would make for a difficult year. It took its toll on me in many ways— and it was no coincidence that it happened the season before my breakdown.

THE BREAKDOWN:
PART EIGHT

SURRENDER

A PSYCHIATRIC HOSPITAL IS SUPPOSED to be the place where you recover from mental problems. Unfortunately, the one I found myself in just made me crazier.

I was taken out of my clothes and put in hospital attire, then locked in a room by myself to cool down. It was hard for me to chill, because I could hear through the walls that I was surrounded by patients who definitely had incredibly severe mental problems.

The patients who were confined to the bottom floor.

It was as low as you could go. And that's where they put *me*.

I was like, "Please, get me to the *top* floor; I'll answer all your questions! Please, I'm serious, something is happening with me being down here on this bottom floor. I promise you, I know all my addresses. All my phone numbers from when I grew up. I can give you all you want to know about my grandparents, my history or whatever, just please don't leave me on this bottom floor."

I was so scared—and then my emotions would switch to extreme anger, thinking I could break out of there, bust through a door, or even a wall. I felt like I was in a cage; I really did. I felt so dehumanized. I felt horrible.

A woman who worked there had some compassion. She worked hard to get through to me and help me through the process. But two other people on the staff? They completely creeped me out. They were watching my every move—and one would come into the room they had me in every few minutes and turn the lights on and off, startling me. I shouted, "Dude! What are you doing? I'm already freaked out!"

I got past the terror. I looked for strength. I looked up to God.

And I spoke to Him.

"Father, God, just hit me with your Holy Spirit," I said. "I feel like I'm in hell right now and maybe I deserve to be here, but I know I'm a good person. I've helped so many people and I have so much more to give—and I feel You have a plan for me to do that.

I know that I'm here for a reason, but if ever You listened to one of my prayers, Father God, listen to this one. I won't do wrong anymore. I surrender."

Like I said earlier, I didn't need to try and save anybody else. At that moment, I needed to save myself. That's why I gave my life to Christ right there: Thirty-two years old in a mental institution at the bottom floor and I felt the Holy Spirit for the first time in my life.

At first, I didn't think It was real—but It was.

Up until that point, I had tried to keep everything under control in my life. I planned my future with a military precision, I tried hard never to make a mistake, and I lived out my dream.

Now, it felt like all that control I had was all a lie. It felt like I had NO control.

So what I did was I just turned that control over to the Lord. I would trust Him with my marriage and my family. I would trust Him with my sanity and my future. I would trust Him with my finances and with putting the right people around me.

From that moment on, I trusted Him with everything.

SHOW AND GO

MY THREE SEASONS WITH THE MAGIC opened up a lot more opportunities for me. For example, I had my own radio show in Orlando, where listeners would call in to talk basketball. It was great, especially when people like my old Heat teammate, Dwyane Wade, would call in and surprise me.

I also started doing more and more speaking engagements at places like Boys and Girls Clubs and elementary schools. The NBA expected us to appear at a certain number of events every year, and while a lot of players shrugged them off as assignments they had to do, I actually volunteered to do more than I was supposed to. I enjoyed speaking to people and wanted to get more experience doing it.

Again, I wanted to grow beyond the court.

On the court, I played as hard as I could as always and I focused on growing my leadership skills within the team. Once I left Miami, I knew how to train, I knew what it took to succeed in the game, so I worked my butt off to show others how it was done. As always, I wanted to lead by example and lead from within.

211

But I still wanted to keep it fun. So, I became the jokester and the dancer—not to mention the party planner. I would organize events by telling players, "Hey, we're doing Monday Night Football, fellas only." Or, "Hey, we're getting the families together; we're going to your house. Or maybe, "Fight party—it's at your house, big fella. You make sure you order all the food!"

This was something I learned from Shaq, because that's what he did for his teammates. He'd have us all over and we wouldn't believe the spread of food that would be laid out for us there. Shaq knew what he was doing. If he wanted the rest of the team to run through a wall for him, he wanted them to know he was there to take care of them along the way.

I challenged the older players to take on that Shaq mindset to help strengthen the team's bonds. When they agreed, I turned around and told the younger guys, "Yo, if you want the OGs to look out for you, you'd better do what they ask. When they call you, I don't care what time it is, you go do what they tell you to do and they'll take care of you for it."

It was about enforcing the culture of our game. And it's not a bullying thing, it's a respect thing. You have to know who you are and how important it is to present yourself in an honorable and dignified way.

With that in mind, I could not look the other way if I saw a young player come in with his pants down, not listening and acting all standoffish. I had to correct him. Someone like that, I'd come at them with, "Hey, I don't care about your edge, I know about that edge. I'm from the same place you're from."

I'd go on. "What are you here to do? Are you here to be tough or are you here to make your money? If you want to make money, let me tell you how to do it—there's a recipe. If you want to be tough, go on out there in the streets. They're going to show you tough. The problem is you're going to be tough and broke. So get real."

I was like a big brother to a lot of these guys. A lot of them were from tough areas like mine, only they didn't have the benefit of being raised by a strong father like I was. That was a problem with a lot of my teammates when I was growing up in the hood—they didn't have positive male role models, and my Pop would step in and try to be that for them.

Now I wanted to do the same for those who were willing to accept my mentoring.

I'm talking about players like Jameer Nelson, who told reporters that he felt like I was a big brother to him. I was proud when he asked me to be a groomsman in his wedding and, later on, our families would take vacations together.

Then there was Marcin Gortat, a tall, skinny guy with a great big smile. Marcin was from Poland and came all the way from playing pro ball in Germany to being an NBA rookie during my last season with the Magic. He could barely speak English and was having trouble adjusting to the NBA—but I believed in him and I told him so.

As Marcin told the press, "I remember one thing…he was always supporting me in my rookie year when everybody was cracking jokes about me. He was the only guy who was always saying I was going to play well one day. He always believed that one day I was going to play on a high level.

"I would say he was a true role model off the court. He gave us examples of what we were supposed to say in the media, what we were supposed to wear before and after games, how we were supposed to act, how we were supposed to prepare for a game."

Marcin only played in six games that season, but I didn't give up on him, even though everybody else was more than willing to. I took him out to dinner and gave him the best advice I could. I also challenged him to answer what was rapidly becoming my catchphrase question....

"What's driving you?"

I began using that question to help players connect with their passion and their heart. If they tapped into what motivated them the most, if they remembered why they were there and what their real goals were, they would perform at their highest level. Whether it was their family, the money, the glitzy NBA lifestyle, if they could identify whatever it was that pushed them forward, it would help them become better.

For my part, what was driving me then, and to this day, is the fact that I do not want to fail. I do not want to lose. I can't go back to where I came from, my family can't go back. We've come too far. I want my kids to achieve more than I did, just as I was blessed enough to achieve more than my parents. What drove me was changing the landscape at a generational level.

Whatever was driving Marcin took him to where he needed to go. He turned it around, although I don't take much credit for it. He had the ability, he just had to get in his comfort zone. He went on to become a starting center for the Phoenix Suns and is still playing NBA ball to this day for the Washington Wizards.

Of course, me being me, I still was very capable of occasionally breaking the standards I tried to set for myself and the younger players on the team. I still had that anger burning inside me, despite all my efforts to grow beyond it, and from time to time, it made its way out.

The most explosive example of that happened when I played against the Seattle SuperSonics—more specifically, against the Sonics' Ray Allen, who would eventually become a ten-time NBA All-Star. We were playing a very physical game against him that night; he was a threat and we were trying to shut him down.

He didn't like it one bit.

And I was the guy he ended up taking out his frustration on. He elbowed me and I came back at him, and the result can still be seen on the Internet today. We came to blows as we spilled into the stands, but the other players managed to pull us apart—and then we both got ejected from the game. That should have been the end of it, but it wasn't for me—I didn't feel like we got to finish what we had started.

So I went after him *off* the court—and the police had to pull us apart this time.

But trust me, I learned my lesson after that—and it was an expensive one. I got a five-game suspension and was fined heavily, losing almost $180,000 on that single incident. As I like to say, nobody wins in a basketball fight—except for the NBA, who ends up collecting six figures from whoever was dumb enough to throw a punch.

I never fought again on the court. But it still boggles

my mind that it doesn't happen more often. Coaches motivate you to play on an edge that's almost animalistic—and you get so pumped up that the energy is hard to contain. So I admire the discipline of all the players who can avoid getting into a mess on the court—especially when trash talk comes into play. You're often getting called every name in the book—and a few that are too rough to be in *any* book, especially mine!—and you have to control how you react.

Whenever you see a player, a player in any professional sport, acting out during the game—or even screaming at the camera in a crazy way afterward—it's almost always the result of that pent-up energy. If you're a viewer sitting on your couch at home watching, you might think, "Wow, that's some scary dude." But often what you're seeing is a release of the extreme emotions a pro player experiences while pushing himself to the limit to succeed.

The Ray Allen story, however, has a happy ending. I believe the next time we saw each other, we met at half-court, gave each other a hug and apologized to each other. I said, "I didn't mean it, I have nothing personal against you." He felt the same way and from that point on, we were good.

When I signed with the Celtics a few years later, who did I suddenly have as my teammate? None other than Ray Allen. We got to know each other a whole lot better through the years and I'm the first one to say that Ray's a great man, an awesome dude, and a strong brother.

During my years with the Magic, my comfort level with the whole NBA experience continued to increase. I began to really enjoy my time in the league—and found that there were three places during the season where I enjoyed the most quality time.

Number one? The locker room. An NBA locker room is like a grown man's playground, filled with people who are extremely wealthy, extremely good at what they do, and in the best shape of their lives—and all from different places around the country and around the world. They're also in a place where they can feel at ease and be completely transparent and honest. The energy is amazing, while the contrasts in personalities and the differences in upbringing make for some weird, fun, and fascinating dynamics. And, of course, it's for guys only.

Number two? On the court for practice. That's where I would work extremely hard—and, at this point, because I was a veteran player, I knew everybody else's job. I could size up the kids on the team, so if one was a step slow, I would let them know. I wouldn't do that based on my perspective, I would do it based on what the coach gave us in his game plan. I would study that game plan and live it on the court until it was second nature, so, again, I could lead by example.

Number three? When you're traveling on the plane or bus to the next city where you're going to play—that's party central. You've got a card game going on in one spot, you've got movies playing in another, you've got the music guys cranking the volume, you've got other guys playing video games…and then there's the older players, sitting at the best table with all the food, calling all the shots.

Me, I would sit a little bit behind people in the middle of the plane so I could read. I would also circulate and check out what was going on everywhere. And there was one other thing I would do on the longer plane rides—and it's not exactly what you might expect from an NBA player during his time off. Actually, it's pretty much the opposite.

I would show the younger guys how to tie a tie.

Yeah, I'd take them through the Double Windsor. And I'd explain it in their language, in lingo they could understand. This might seem funny, but again, a lot of these guys didn't have a dad to teach them this stuff. That's why I would say, "This knot I'm showing you today, I'm not doing this for you, I'm doing this for your grandson—because this is the knot *your* son is going to teach him, because you were able to teach your son how to do it. So I'm doing this for your grandboy, all right?"

Again, for me, it was about changing the generational landscape. We shouldn't want our grandkids wearing white tees like we had to; we should strive for them to be *suited* and *booted*.

Learning to tie a tie was a small thing, but an important thing, the kind of thing I liked to help young players with. They know they can't go to coaches or management with certain life issues—so I always wanted to be there for those guys and, of course, they knew I would keep these talks strictly confidential.

During the end of my second season with the Magic, Tosha and I were blessed with the birth of our third daughter, Jordan Keyan. I was proud of the family my beautiful wife and I were growing.

The team was also doing awesome. Each year, our record improved. The last two seasons I was with them, we made it to the playoffs (and both times we were eliminated by the Pistons in postseason, just as the Heat had the year I was with them—you don't mess with Detroit!).

But shadows were beginning to fall in other areas.

During my third and final season in Orlando—the eighth year of my NBA career—I felt like I was in my prime. Stan Van Gundy had come over from the Heat to coach the team, which was awesome. I was increasingly getting respect around the league as a player and it was a very good point in my career. I was happy with my role in the union and excited to continue mentoring those around me. But what goes up must come down.

I was sucker-punched by the news that I had a potentially huge physical problem—a degenerative hip that meant I was a high risk when it came to incurring serious injuries. The Magic didn't want to sign me again with that situation hanging over me.

Worse than that—much worse than that—Pop was sick again, and this time it was much more severe than his stroke.

My original mentor, my most important leader, the man who influenced me above all other men, was diagnosed with prostate cancer. And the long-term outlook was not good.

"SHOOT IT, BUBBA!"

IT WAS MY NINTH SEASON in the NBA and I was playing the best ball of my life. I had signed a two-year deal with the New Jersey Nets, with an option for a third, and posted career highs in points, assists, and minutes per game. The Nets were trying a new "dribble-drive" offense and I loved it.

How good was my game? Well, remember that Clippers coach who told me I wasn't going to make it in the NBA? He came up to me that year and said, "Hey, man, I'm proud of you. You proved me wrong. See how much I know?"

That was sweet. But I didn't have much time to savor that turnaround. Those shadows—my Pop's sickness and my own hip problem—were growing. And soon both threw a lot of darkness our way, along with another dose of misfortune I never even saw coming.

The worst year of my life began during the first week of November 2008. Tosha and I were expecting our fourth child; this time, we were hopeful it would be a boy. Nothing against our beautiful girls, but every dad loves to have a son

221

of his own. Unfortunately, during this time, Tosha lost the baby. That hit her hard. I didn't talk about it much, but it shook me to the core as well. I just didn't have time to linger on it; I had to play a game the next night and I did.

That Christmas, my folks came up to our New Jersey home for the holidays. For the most part, it was a great time—but there was a sadness underneath it all, because it seemed as though it might be Pop's last Christmas. His cancer was spreading and his condition continued to decline. He was feeling so poorly, he ended up having to see a doctor in New Jersey before going back home to Florida.

When you're in the middle of a season, however, you can't spend too much energy on worrying about outside concerns. When you're a pro, it's essential to focus to keep your competitive edge and I had to keep playing ball as hard as I could. Our lost child and my sick father, however, haunted the back corridors of my mind and tore at my spirit—and I also knew that my hip would have to be attended to sooner rather than later.

In February 2010 came the one bright spot of that time, a very bright spot: Tosha found out she was pregnant again. When all the tests indicated the baby would be healthy, I danced with joy—as a matter of fact, in my very next game, I scored more than 20 points.

The team finished up the season doing okay, but placed third in the division and didn't make the playoffs. Although I'd had a career year, I wished we'd done better as a team. I hoped next season we would improve.

I also hoped I would be still be able to play.

A few days after our last game, I finally went in for

arthroscopic hip surgery at the Hospital for Special Surgery in New York City. Even though the team had hooked me up with one of the top three hip surgeons in the country, you never knew if an operation of that magnitude was going to work out.

I stayed in the hospital to recover, because there was also an amazing physical therapist there that would be a big help to my rehabilitation. That meant I couldn't really travel to spend time with Pop, even though he was getting sicker and sicker. He made it to his sixtieth birthday party about a month after my surgery, but, on June 20, 2009, my father was gone.

For me, that loss was catastrophic.

Leroy Dooling II, my father, was the face I always looked for in the stands, from the time I was five years old and playing on my first basketball team to the NBA games he was able to attend. When he couldn't make it to a game, we always made it a point to talk on the phone before the opening tip-off. This constant motivating presence was forever gone from my life.

Nobody would be yelling, "Shoot it, Bubba!" ever again.

He passed in the condo I had bought for him and my mom. When I got the news, we all cried together as a family, including our kids. Pop wasn't just a hands-on dad, he was a hands-on granddad and the impact of his death was huge on our household.

We traveled back to the old neighborhood for his funeral, which became a major community event. My dad, as I've detailed, was a very prominent figure—so revered that the church couldn't even hold all the people that wanted to get in and say goodbye to him. One of my buddies from high school had his own funeral home by then, so he took care of all the arrangements and did a very good job. I was grateful for how he handled everything with honor, dignity, and respect. It was tough for him, because when he was a kid he had spent a lot of time with me and my dad.

My brother, Leroy, also did his part. He had started his own floral business, the third Leroy Dooling to do so. He did the casket spray because he was very gifted with flowers; my father taught that skill to him. It was nice to see that torch passed on.

As for me, I never felt like I had the opportunity to properly grieve for my father, just as I didn't get the time to grieve for the baby that Tosha had lost months before. Others had the freedom to fall apart, and rightfully so. But I was given no space to emotionally deal with burying the most important man in my life, the guy who had always been my number one supporter.

Instead, the funeral, for me, was a grueling ordeal.

As I related earlier in this book, one of the big shocks I experienced when I became an NBA player was that suddenly everyone I knew was looking to me for handouts. Well, that all reached its peak at the funeral. When I was back in the hood, I got asked for more than $100,000 from different people—at one of my lowest points in my life. Again, no one seemed to care about the pain I was going through.

It was a repeat of what had happened when, during my first few NBA seasons, I returned to my hometown every summer to run a basketball camp for boys. My father had helped mentor many kids without dads and I wanted to follow in his footsteps. The problem was, every year, more and more people showed up to swamp me with requests, leaving me unable to focus on the thing I had come there to do. Even though it was a project I was passionate about, there was no way to keep it going.

Now it was happening again. My heart hurt. After the funeral was over and we left to go back to New Jersey, I had to fight off the bitterness and resentment that was threatening to overwhelm me. Most of that negativity was swept away a few months later, on October 11, when our son, Keyon LaTwae Dooling Jr., was born. Little KJ was a big blessing in our lives just when we needed it most.

There was one more pleasant surprise in store for me. When I was about to return to the court for the first time after my father's passing, I got a phone call right before game time. Only this time it wasn't my dad doing his traditional pregame motivational call—no, it was my big brother, Eric, doing a dead-on impression of how Pop used to do it.

It was good to connect with my dad's spirit in that way one last time.

BATTLE FOR POSITION

MY SECOND YEAR with the Nets was...well, interesting.

First of all, we started the 2009-2010 season by setting a new NBA record—only it wasn't a good one. Nobody had ever gone 0 and 18 before. Yep, we lost our first eighteen games in a row. The funny thing was our first win came when I played for the first time that season!

I missed the first five weeks or so, because I was still recovering from the hip surgery. I didn't feel good at all. But I also knew I had a job to do; I had to prove that I still had it, so I could get another contract. The Nets had the option to drop me after this season and, if they ended up not wanting me, I definitely wanted another chance with another team. So the pressure was on again.

Luckily, I had an ally in my fight to get back to full playing strength. The Nets had an amazing trainer, a Jersey boy named Tim Walsh who had been with the team for ten years. Tim loved to listen to another Jersey boy—a guy by the name of Frank Sinatra—so he'd play Frank's greatest hits every time I worked with him.

Because Tim and I spent so much time together, we ended up talking a whole lot about everything under the sun—family, our upbringing, and most of all, basketball. Tim had been around the NBA for more than thirty years at that point, and he had a lot of great inside stories to relate that only basketball people got to share with each other.

Having that positive bond with Tim helped a great deal when I was still recovering. When your livelihood depends on your physical well-being, it's easy to feel down about the implications of being hurt. Having somebody like Tim around to cheer me up made all the difference.

So, yeah, I finally got back on the court for our first win of the season, nineteen games in. But if you think I can take any credit for turning the team around with my brilliant, masterful playing, think again—because things only got worse as the season wore on.

On December 26, we became the sixth team in NBA history to lose twenty-eight of its first thirty games, tying the worst thirty-game record ever. On January 23, we became the third team in NBA history to lose forty of its first forty-three games. On February 6, we went for the triple crown and got it. We lost that night and our record went to 4–46, which tied the record the for worst fifty-game record in the history of the three major sports (basketball, baseball, and hockey) that play seasons that long. For the season, we ended up 12–70.

In case you were wondering, no, we did not make the playoffs.

WHAT'S DRIVING YOU???

Now, you read all that and the amount of games we lost almost seems funny. Well, it ain't so funny when you go through it. Adding to the overall chaos was a bunch of coaching changes. After the first sixteen consecutive losses, the head coach was fired and his assistant took over for a couple of games. Then the general manager of the team took over as head coach. Nothing turned it around. It was just another part of my horrible, awful, no good year.

On the positive side, my body responded well to the surgery. I knew I had played as well as I was capable of while I was still recovering and that I'd be a lot better the next season. Then I'd be back at 100 percent.

But I didn't know where I'd *be* next season.

The Nets left me hanging until the last minute. With one day left to pick up my option, they decided to cut me loose. But at the very least, I got a nice send-off from sports columnist Dave D'Alessandro of the *New Jersey Star-Ledger.* Under a headline that read, "A classy departure for Nets guard Keyon Dooling," he wrote:

> *It is our earnest hope that after [the Nets] get through the arduous process of roster building, the Nets find at least one guy like Keyon Dooling—in other words, an adult presence who puts the team first and embraces the responsibility of being the voice of its collective spirit... being around him is like cracking open your first bottle of champagne: He is a one-man pep rally, and the kind of leader who makes a locker room a better place.*

229

With all the knowledge I had gained from my experience serving on the NBPA board, I decided to go ahead and negotiate whatever my next deal would be all by myself. Luckily, the Milwaukee Bucks needed a backup guard and were happy to have me.

Well, at least most of them were....

RESET

I SPENT ONE SEASON with the Bucks, and for the most part, it was a fun experience. I got to play in more games than any other season and, although the team didn't do spectacularly well, it was certainly an improvement over the previous year with the Nets.

But I did hit one big roadblock that season.

At this late point in my career, going into my eleventh season, I was entering the rarified atmosphere that only a real NBA long-timer gets to breathe. I thought that experience was a plus to my teammates on the Bucks. Besides helping them to understand the importance of the union, I worked hard to help keep the mood positive, the team motivated, and the competitive edge in place. And, as always, I mentored any players who might be going through some personal stuff and need someone to help them through whatever was going on.

Most players responded enthusiastically to my mentorship. Since I spoke their language and had a good reputation in the league, they felt free to approach me with the realest of the real stuff. They would come to me with a serious issue and I would work to connect them with the best possible resources through the union. It could be a drug problem, a tax problem, 401k stuff, or just understanding what their rights were regarding contracts and free agency. Whatever the case, I would dive in and do what I could. I really loved these young guys and I wanted them to know more about things than I did at their age. It was simply paying it forward from those who had mentored me.

But, for the first time, some of the guys weren't receptive. They didn't understand what I was about and the more I tried to help them, the more they rebelled against me. Maybe it was because I had just turned thirty—maybe I was suddenly too old to trust for some reason. I don't know. But the tension was building.

Finally, one day during practice, it all came to a head.

The younger players just started laughing at me, ragging on me about everything I did. It was, "Why do you run so hard? Why are you always on time? Why do you work so hard? Why do you dress like that? Why do you speak to everybody? That's some ho-ass s–t."

They were actually calling me a "company man." Me— a company man? *Me?*

What's funny is that some of the same people who dissed me came to me for help later. I'm still helping them now—which is all I wanted to do in the first place. At the time, however, I was very upset at being rejected at that level. I was so upset that, when we were traveling by jet to our next road game, I spent a good deal of time composing the following note to myself:

Today is the day! Thirty years old and hungry as ever. As I fly across the country, I reflect on a million things: Unorganized noises, sounds, thoughts, insecurities, pain, confidence, swag, joy, peace, anger, hope...I could go on and on.

So here's my way of expressing myself to me: Be honest with yourself in these writings. Growth is mandatory when you are responsible for many. And before I write anything else—to God be the glory!!

As a man, I wanna leave a legacy. Yeah, everyone says that, but at an early age, I knew I was a go-getter. Thanks, Bubba, for putting all that swag in me. As a man, I gotta be willing to not only live for my fam, but die for them.

Loyalty comes and goes, depending on what phase of life you are in. Loyalty without a purpose or a common interest can bring confusion. If a crew, your inner circle, your homies, etc., don't grow together, eventually it will fall apart by holding onto the threads of the past!

Through the years, I have given sooo much and it never seems to be enough. My life has taken the pattern of selflessness to a fault. As that snowball effect takes shape, I grow a sense of isolation, loneliness, coldness—alongside grit, determination, and responsibility. Weird, right?

See, what I've come to realize is that I'm built for this! I go harder when the average cat relaxes. Yep, there's that ambition as a rider again. Life experience has been my best teacher; I only wish I could have learned more without having to go through it, but the cycle is broken now because my kids will be so much more equipped than me and Tosha.

Toughness means a lot to me. I feel like the weak will be conquered because they lack that trait. A part of me says they will get what they deserve, while another part me says, "Protect them, help them, lead them." Where I sit now, I know that everyone ain't built Ford Tough, but, if they are led by the right person, they can find their way and be productive with the right structure in place. I embrace my alpha male personality and want every man to be able to feel that power in their own realm.

As another hoop season nears its end, I ask myself, have I gotten better? Have I grown? Have I helped someone get better as a person or uplifted someone at a vulnerable moment? Yep—but I still wanna do it on a larger scale. Question: With so many layers to my personality, how do I organize my direction?

Tonight was a weird night. I was tarred and feathered by my teammates for being everything that they are not. "Hahaha, man, you stretch too much, you run too hard, you speak too much to everyone, why you dress like that? Man, you tryin' to act like a coach?" I was offended initially, but now I understand. People will try to make your best attributes into flaws, because they lack skills in those areas.

Maybe I shouldn't be too helpful? Should I stop paying it forward because people don't get me? Hahaha, hell no! I'm the same dude everyday and I love that about me! Those same people will need me one day and I will not hold it against them if they are worthy of help. With people outside of your inner circle, you need to live by logic and rules, not feelings and emotions.

What I wrote on the plane that day became my manifesto; it wasn't a polished and perfect piece of writing, but it was what was pouring out of my heart. That was the day

WHAT'S DRIVING YOU???

I decided, in spite of what had happened with the players who were mocking me, that I would continue to use the ability I had to mentor others and help them lead better lives. As a matter of fact, I would make it an even bigger part of my life.

That was the day I decided what I would be doing after I left the NBA.

TIME-OUT

WHO DEFINES YOU?

Yeah, I know the title of this book is "What's driving you?"—but this is another critical question to ask yourself too. And before you answer it, think about everybody who *wants* to define you.

Start with everyone who's personally close to you. They may be great people (and I hope they are), but *they* still want you to be what they want you to be, so that the relationship works best for them. That's just how people are and it's something that took me a long time to work out. I always want to give my best to every situation and I never want to disappoint anyone. But some people always want too much.

Now, move on to those whose actual *job* it is to define you. If you're in school, these people would be your teachers, professors, guidance counselors, even administrators in certain situations. If you work, you have a boss that has to make the call on you; if you provide a service, you have clients passing judgment on how good you are at what you're doing for them. Or, if you're an athlete like I was, you have everybody from teammates to coaches to club presidents to fans constantly assessing who you are and what you can do.

The truth is, *everybody* you encounter attempts to define you. That's simple human nature—we size up people so we can make sense of them. Even the FedEx guy who's delivering a package might make a snap judgment that you're a loser, just because you're wearing a ratty bathrobe when you come to the door. Of course, he can't have that big of an impact on your life, so it's nothing to worry about.

But the other people I mentioned? They can have an immense impact on whether you succeed or you fail, whether you're happy or depressed, whether you pursue your passions, or don't bother to try. Some of those people will lift you up—others will bring you down. Some will add to your life—others will only try to take.

So be careful to take a close look at who's trying to define you—because some will try to put you in a box you'll find it hard to break out of.

From the beginning, I never trusted others' negative assessments of me. I knew what I could do—but, at the same time, it was up to me to prove it. I didn't let them define me. Instead, I was determined to show my talent on the court. Dillard High School told me I couldn't play varsity? I went to Cardinal Gibbons and played varsity. My college coach told me I couldn't shoot? I played my heart out to prove him wrong. An NBA coach told me I wasn't good enough for the pros? I came back with a vengeance.

WHAT'S DRIVING YOU???

I defined myself. Because I *had* to, in order to achieve what I wanted to achieve.

Now, my definition of myself could have been wrong. But if I *had* been wrong, I wouldn't have lasted thirteen years in the NBA. To be sure, I was never a superstar player, but I found my place and I'm proud of how I served the game on the court then—and off the court now.

My point is, the people who try to define you don't know enough about you to have the final say. Only *you* do. Yes, be realistic about who you are and what you can do, but, at the same time, never stop testing your abilities to see how far you can go, and never stop trying to transcend any limitations you might feel being imposed on you by others.

For my part, I've learned it's crucial to seek out honest feedback from positive mentors who have the vital experience and knowledge that enables them to assess what I already have—and what I need to gain to reach the next level of whatever endeavor I'm pursuing. I've also learned in my mentoring that it's important to give the other person as positive a definition as possible, while being honest and giving them the tools to improve. Build people up, don't knock them down.

The truth is, the definition of who you are should always be changing and evolving. You should always be moving toward your next step and the next level.

That's why you shouldn't let others define you. Because they're just looking at where you are at the moment—not what you have the potential of becoming.

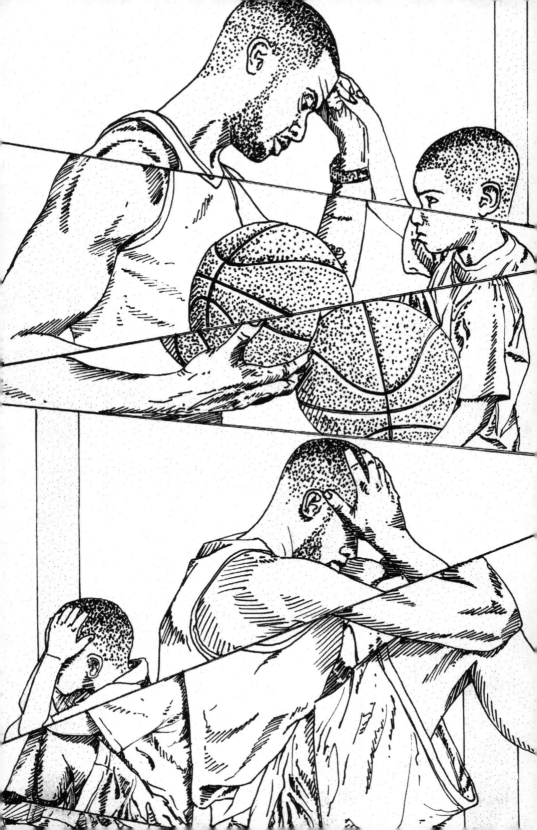

THE BREAKDOWN:
PART NINE

LOOKING TO GET OUT

I FINALLY GOT OFF THE BOTTOM FLOOR.

It took a few hours of being trapped in what felt like hell, but I was finally moved up a few floors and into my own room at the psychiatric hospital. I was assigned a social worker, a counselor, and a nurse.

They told me about some classes I could go to in order to start recovering, but I didn't want to go. I didn't want to be around anyone. I was hallucinating, belligerent, and paranoid. And, for some reason, I felt really cold. I just couldn't get warm.

I wasn't getting better.

First of all, they didn't seem interested in why I had cracked up. They just wanted me to be okay. They never asked what the cause of what I was going through was.

Second of all, the meds they had me on were actually making things worse. They put me on some stuff I shouldn't have been on, designed to treat high blood pressure. Well, I never had high blood pressure before—it was probably only a temporary condition caused by my freak-out. As for the meds I was supposed to be on? I later found out that they were giving me *four times* the dosage that I should have been taking.

The mixture wasn't good, to say the least.

The worst part was that they gave me my meds just before visiting hours. And because they did the exact opposite of calming me down, because they revved me up in completely the wrong direction, I was on my worst behavior when people came to visit.

That's why, when Tosha was finally able to see me, she didn't know what to make of me. Her husband, the father of her four children, seemed like he was slipping away for good.

I also had a surprise visitor: Doc Rivers.

Doc had flown back to his home in Florida for the weekend—but he did so with an uneasy feeling about me. Doc and I were very close. He knew me and he saw how I was when I showed up at the Celtics' offices, talking about quitting the game. He knew I wasn't right.

At the time, both of us were serving on the NBA competition committee, a group of owners, coaches, and players that dealt with NBA game rules. We determined if any changes needed to happen and how those changes should be worded and implemented. Well, because of my breakdown, I was a no-show on a conference call meeting of the committee during that weekend.

That set alarm bells off in Doc's head—and he immediately flew back up to Boston to track me down. Once he found me, he came to see me every day, bless him. I told him I didn't want to let down the team. He listened patiently and gave me the support I needed, even though he had no idea what was going on with me.

Soon, he did.

Tosha and Doc were the first two people I finally revealed my secret to—the secret I had kept inside for decades. The secret that kept an anger burning in me. The secret that fueled my internal low shot clock for so many years. I told them about the molestation.

At first, Tosha didn't believe me. She thought I was still tripping. I understood that, with all the crazy stuff I had been spouting. But she made a call to the person I told her to call, and she immediately had the incident confirmed.

Meanwhile, behind the scenes, what I didn't know was that other family members who had heard about my situation were suddenly out to take advantage of it. I won't name names, but they were after power of attorney over me—meaning they could control what happened to me, as well as my money!

More betrayal. That was just what I didn't need.

And Tosha certainly deserved better. This was at a time when she had her hands full and then some. She was dealing with a husband who still wasn't right in the head being treated in a place she didn't trust. At the same time, she was caring for four children who didn't know what had happened to daddy. And then, on top of all that, she was blindsided with this insulting and terrifying legal maneuvering.

Meanwhile, Doc had called Billy Hunter, the head of the NBPA, to help get me out of that facility. Doc could tell they weren't doing right by me—the vibe of the place really shook him up. He said to me, "We've got to get you the f—out of here." I agreed, but I didn't know if I should leave.

It was Thursday. I had been there a few days and I still kept feeling cold, so, all week, I had always sat in the sunlight to try and warm up. Well, this particular day, there was a group that was going outside on the grounds and I got very excited—I could get out directly in the sun and get that heat streaming down on me. In my state, this was a big thing to look forward to.

And, wouldn't you know it, that's just when they called me in for my evaluation.

I was like, "Oh my God, why call me now? I want to go outside! I want to go outside!" But thank God, I didn't put up a fight. Because I was about to get my key to freedom.

At my evaluation, they told me I was in that facility *voluntarily*. In other words, since I had committed myself, since I had *asked* to go to a psychiatric hospital…well, I could leave any time I wanted. I don't know if Doc and Billy pushed for them to make this clear to me or not, but they did.

At first, I didn't know what to do with that information. My head was still foggy and, again, I thought maybe I needed to stay. I couldn't think straight and I didn't know enough about what I was going through.

Then, Tosha came to see me and told me about the power of attorney situation. She told me I had to get out of there and fight for her and the kids—and myself. She said, "Baby, you've got to come up out of this thing! I need you."

Suddenly, the clouds parted. Suddenly, my head cleared up. Suddenly, the meds didn't matter anymore. I snapped out of it because I saw the threat to my loved ones. I was livid and I knew what I had to do. The first thing the next day, Friday, I told the facility I wanted out.

Next bad surprise. I had to wait until Monday—because they needed one business day to process my request!

Because I was now focused, I used that weekend to start getting healthy. I began exercising, I walked on the treadmill, I forced myself to eat, and started going to the classes the facility suggested. I even switched back into my old mode of trying to motivate others; patients wanted to come and work out with me, so I did pushups with them and encouraged *them* to get better.

I was going to come back from this. I had to—or I could lose everything.

LOCKOUT

TWO YEARS BEFORE I JOINED THE NBA, the basketball season was reduced to only fifty games. The 1998-1999 season was probably best known for a lockout that lasted more than six months. Everyone knew about it, but since I was in college at the time, I was lucky enough not to have to deal with it.

Now, it was 2011 and I wasn't so lucky.

Our 2005 CBA, the one that Shaq and the rest of the Heat had schooled me on, had expired. We weren't asking for more from the NBA; no, they wanted us to take less than we already had. The 2005 CBA had supposedly hurt the owners of teams in smaller cities, and those owners wanted that ship turned around.

The NBA made it clear which way the new deal had to go. During the year leading up to the expiration of the 2005 agreement, the owners weren't seriously bargaining. Instead, they were getting all their ducks in a row for the lockout. It's not as if they were sneaky about it—it was straight up and very transparent. They wanted things to change and they were going to fight as hard and for as long as they needed to get us to cave.

We wanted to fight back just as hard.

At the same time, we offered some concessions—but the NBA didn't think we were putting enough on the table. Despite urgent last-minute negotiations the night of June 30, NBA commissioner, David Stern, and Billy Hunter, the head of the NBPA, both announced that the sides were too far apart to come to an agreement.

On July 1, the lockout began.

During a lockout, as most of you reading this already know, the players are frozen out of the game. Teams are not allowed to trade, sign, or even to contact players. While the lockout continued, we also weren't allowed to use any NBA facilities or have access to NBA trainers or staff. And we would start getting hit hard in our wallets if the lockout went beyond November 15, which was the date of the first paycheck of the season.

By this time, I was first vice president of the union, behind only the president, Derek Fisher of the Lakers. It was a pressure-packed position to be in; players' livelihoods were at stake as were the revenues of the owners. On both sides, there was some dissension in the ranks—people were panicking over how much money they were going to lose and wanted the lockout to end by any means necessary.

Tense times. I had a steady stream of phone calls from players who wanted a continual update on negotiations. Most were worried not only about taking care of their own families, but other people they were supporting with their player salaries. I had that to deal with on my end; even if I wasn't getting a paycheck from the NBA, those that I took care of still wanted *their* checks.

Ironically, I was busier than ever during the lockout, and not just with the constant union meetings with lawyers and NBA representatives. I was determined to take advantage of this time off by expanding my off-the-court activities in the directions I saw my post-player career going.

One important step was my becoming an ambassador for the GameTyme foundation. Working with GameTyme changed my life, because not only did I get to organize these events, down to ordering the goods we would donate, but I also was able to build relationships with the vendors and local community leaders.

I did a lot of things I had never done before—which was dope, because I gained confidence in these new abilities. I also got to improve my speaking skills by emceeing these events and doing a media tour in each city we visited to bring attention to our charity. Finally, because I partnered with other NBA guys to help out their communities, they were very appreciative. That strengthened the bonds I had with them.

And, most importantly, we were helping people in places plagued by poverty. I felt I was doing what I call Kingdom work. It was all mission work to me, even the union work. There, I was fighting for the players and the families of the workers who weren't getting paid because no NBA games were being played. That was important to me.

I also found a way to expand my business knowledge. I went to San Antonio, Texas and interned with a CEO who was worth almost $300 million. This guy was a major donor to the GameTyme Foundation and a major distributor. He invited me out to study his whole operation and learn how businesses work at that level. He helped me, and, luckily enough, I was able to really help him as well. I gave him structure, coached a lot of the people in his office, and made a few dollars along the way. And again, I was proud of the impact I was able to make. I mean, I helped him improve his margins—who knew I knew about margins? Damn!

And, to be honest, my role in the lockout itself even helped me widen my horizons; as I say, the good comes with the bad. I was given an almost exclusive 360-degree view of the organization and access to an incredible network of people. Not only did I get to watch masters of negotiation like David Stern, but, because the lockout was going through all these nasty legal twists and turns, I was involved with secret meetings with David Boies, one of the biggest litigators in the country. Then there were the journalists, the top ones in the country, who were constantly pumping insiders like me for information about the lockout. I couldn't give them much (if any) of that information, but I did establish important connections.

And being in these kinds of high-level meetings made me feel so alive. Again, I was a kid from the hood who never saw himself having a window into this world, let alone being a big part of it; it let me know that I've got what it takes. I was like, "You mean I understand all this? You mean to tell me I know all about collective bargaining? You mean to tell me I know all of our benefits? You mean to tell me I know the difference between the mid-level exception, the biannual exception, and the cap? How did this happen?"

It happened by being present.

I was there and I took notes. And I saw that if you said something two years before and you were now contradicting yourself, David Stern would call you on it. We were in a room full of lawyers, so every word you said you were bound to and every word *they* said was crafted to give them an enormous amount of wiggle room.

I read and learned from important books like *The 48 Laws of Power* and *The Art of War*—but I didn't really have to. All that strategy and more was on display during negotiations. Once I saw all those principles in action, I thought, "Okay, I am in the room with some extraordinary human beings." And it made me study more and find out more. I educated myself in a way I had never done.

Despite all that good stuff, I can't sugarcoat the trauma of the lockout. The stress of it all came at me from different directions. The preseason was cancelled and we ended up hitting that watershed date when our first paychecks were due. They didn't come, and all games through December 15 ended up getting cancelled too. Everybody was freaking. Some days I might get twenty calls from twenty different players, who just wanted to come back and play. I was one of the guys they vented their frustrations on.

There were also huge and destructive internal conflicts within the union. People didn't trust each other and some were accused of working with the NBA. I won't speak to all that, only to say that I served as honorably as I could, even as I watched our NBPA implode.

Finally, there was *my* wife and kids. They were very tense about what was going to happen and I wasn't there that much to help soothe their nerves. The charity work and the union meetings were keeping me on the road almost as much as a normal NBA season—and I should have been around more, as I found out later.

But my low shot clock was still ticking loudly. Maybe more loudly than ever.

I felt compelled to keep moving, growing, and building. Even when the lockout ended, I still didn't know how much time I had left as a player. Obviously, I was getting older and I was dealing with a degenerative hip, so I knew the end was coming. I *really* wanted to get paid while I still could—but, as a union officer, my duties meant I had to hang tough and fight for everybody else. We couldn't just take any deal, we had to get the best deal we could. I was willing to lose my entire year's salary to make sure the next generation would be able to feed their family the way I was able to feed mine.

In the end, I'm proud of the work I did for the union, I'm proud of the integrity I brought to the table, and I'm very proud of the way I fought for our guys. The difficult part is the chaotic mess our union ended up in. I don't even like to think about it, let alone talk about it, to this day.

When people ask me how long the lockout went, I tell them, "Four paychecks." That's how we measured the time. We got paid every other week, so you can do the math. On November 25, we resumed negotiations with the league and, on the next day, after fifteen hours of talks, a deal was reached. Maybe Santa was in on the deal, because our season finally started on Christmas Day. We would play a reduced season, cutting our usual eighty-two games to only sixty-six games.

The final losses, not only to us, but to those who worked for the teams and in the arenas we played, were substantial. Everybody got hurt. Even the TV channels that carried NBA games lost an estimated $1 billion in commercial revenue.

I was glad it was all over, but I was tired—not a good place to be in *before* the season started. Fortunately, I was in for a happy surprise that would not only re-energize me, but also bring me one of my most fulfilling years playing ball.

The Bucks had traded me to the Celtics.

UBUNTO

WHEN THE LOCKOUT ENDED, I was still a Milwaukee Buck. Two weeks later, I was a Celtic. Boston needed a backup for Rajon Rondo, coming off his first All-Star season. I was more than happy to be picked for the job.

No NBA franchise has won as many championships as the Boston Celtics. And few are as respected and honored. I was once again part of one of the great organizations in basketball, just as I had been with the Heat.

Unbelievable.

It was my most incredible year as a pro. I got to play with some of the legends of the game—the kind of team I would have created for myself if I was playing NBA Live or NBA 2K on the Xbox. Kevin Garnett, Walter Ray Allen, Paul Pierce…they were all future Hall of Famers.

And then there was Doc Rivers.

As I mentioned earlier in this book, he was one of three men in the NBA who were the most important to my development as a person and a player. Doc had an impact on players even if they didn't ever play for him. All you had to do was just watch him, because he was a walking example of what you could be if you did things right.

What I loved about him was that he didn't sweat the small things. If you didn't want to practice in a shirt, you didn't have to. If you wanted to listen to your music on the plane, you could go ahead. He wasn't tripping off dress code or anything that didn't impact the big picture.

But when you had a job to do in the weight room, on the court, in a professional setting? It was, "Do your f—ing job!"

That's because he had only one team rule—and it only had one word in it: *Respect.* Respect your trainer's time. You have a massage set up, be there on time. Respect the equipment guys' job—don't leave your stuff all raggedy, put it in the bin. The message was that people worked hard for us—and we should do our part to help them do what they did for us. Doc held you accountable.

Doc was consistent, he was passionate, he was compassionate, he was articulate, and he was tough. All you had to do was listen to his thunderous voice to know you didn't mess. To me, he was everything that you would want to be as a man.

And as a coach. After an outstanding thirteen year run as an NBA player, he moved into coaching. He had been coaching for a little more than ten years when I joined the team. He had already won two Eastern Conference championships, and one NBA championship. He had also been NBA Coach of the Year and the NBA All-Star Game head coach twice. Today, he's doing an incredible job with my first NBA team, the Clippers.

When I came to the Celtics, I was still deeply missing my

Pop, even though it had been two years since he passed. I finally found a new father figure in Doc. When I needed guidance from an older man, someone who had more experience than me in life, Doc was there. I had been suffering without my dad's wisdom, strength, and love, and Doc helped ease that pain with his leadership and skill.

He also gave the best pregame speeches I had ever heard in my life. It wasn't the standard pep talk by any means. No, Doc would pull directly from his life experience and be honest and direct—as well as show his vulnerability. Many of his stories were about *his* father, who was a police officer, and the lessons he learned from him. He would take you on an emotional roller coaster, from the bottom to the top and back down again, and I would see these legendary basketball greats getting all pumped up. As for me, I would just try to contain myself; in the middle of one of his talks, I just wanted to yell, "Let me out there now! Please let me out there now! You don't have to say anything else, Doc, just let me out there now!"

Maybe the most important aspect of his leadership was his use of the philosophy of Ubuntu, a South African term popularized by the iconic Nelson Mandela. Ubuntu doesn't have one simple meaning, but it's a word that signifies respect, unselfishness, sharing, and community. The idea is that, "In order for me to be all I can be, I need you to be all you can be—so that we can be all the best *we* can be." Doc would say that if you applied Ubuntu in your house, at your job, in your community, in your county, if you apply it *everywhere* you go, you can impact the whole world and make it a better place.

KEYON L. DOOLING

How important was Ubuntu to the Celtics? Well, when Doc took the team to the 2008 NBA championship, that word was inscribed into their championship rings.

However, for most of the season, we were not allowed to say the word. Why? Because Doc would exclaim loudly, "We're not there yet!" In other words, we had not achieved that bond as a team. I didn't get it. I didn't know why we couldn't say it when the team had already been known for Ubuntu for the last four years.

It wasn't until we were getting close to the playoffs that he finally thought we had achieved Ubuntu. I know I had. I gave myself to the team in a way I hadn't since I played with Miami. I was through worrying about getting my next player contract; I was an older player and I just didn't care anymore. I just wanted to do for the team. And Doc let me do just that in a way I had never been allowed before.

It began with my mentorship of Rajon Rondo. Before coming to Boston, I was a little wary of him. I had heard so many stories about how tough he was to work with and how hard he was to talk to—I just didn't know what I was in for. His reputation was that he was standoffish, super smart, and super emotional—but, I had to say, these are the characteristics of many great men. Most great men, they hate authority and they hate the system and they're very passionate about their beliefs, because they see a better way. Rondo was also a super-competitive guy: He wanted to win the drills, he wanted to win at playing checkers, heck, he even wanted to win at Connect Four. If you've ever seen the video of him taking down two ESPN guys in two separate games at once, you know what I'm talking about.

WHAT'S DRIVING YOU???

So here I was, on a mission to connect with this supposedly scary dude everyone's talking about. I didn't really have a choice, they even moved his locker next to mine to get the relationship going.

Result? A great friendship.

I found him to be the total *opposite* of scary. I think the timing had a lot to with it —he was at a place in life where he was open to my way of helping. There were a lot of misconceptions about him in the media and even in the league, and I wanted people to appreciate Ray (that's what I call him) for who he truly was.

And who is he? An amazing player and an amazing guy. I can count on the fingers of one hand the number of NBA players that I seriously consider to be true friends that I can always depend on. Ray is one of them—a man of quality.

Unlike the Bucks, the Celtics were receptive to who I was as a person and allowed me to become the ultimate hype man. I was called the "emotional center" of the team by *The Boston Globe*—but I became that largely because Doc Rivers allowed me to be that person. It got to the point with him where, if he had a message to deliver to a player, I would be the guy to deliver it. He didn't need to talk to them, he would just let me know what had to be communicated.

It began about halfway through the season. He would go, "Keyon! Rondo's not here with us tonight, I need you to get him going." Or, "Paul's mind isn't right. Turn him around." Or, "Tell Kevin to get on the block, we need him to score." He would say these things and just walk away. So, again—no choice for me. I had to get in there and tell all-time greats to do better!

261

KEYON L. DOOLING

While Doc was manning the huddle, I was left with the responsibility to tell these guys what he wanted from them. And somehow it worked. He knew they didn't want to hear his voice all the time and that I had the years and the leadership quality that would make them want to listen to me. So he leaned on me. He'd say, "I need the bench ready when you come in!"—and I would run practice. We would do drills and make everyone go "game speed," because when we go in, we need to go in together. These were fun times, fun times.

But nothing was more fun than flexin'.

Me and Marquis Daniels, another Florida boy, would do a goofy straight-up-and-down fist pump with both arms when we were warming the bench, to keep the team hyped during a game and to acknowledge a great play. It was no big thing. Then, late one night, a few of us were watching a game, something we would do on the road because we'd be too revved up from a game to sleep. One of my teammates noticed our moves, turned to me and said, "KD, what was this you were doing when you were out there?" And I was like, "I don't know. We were just flexin' on them."

It wasn't anything all that spectacular, it was the kind of move you'd see in music videos and the like, but it suddenly caught on. We turned around and suddenly everybody in the stands at a home game was doing it! It grew to the point where the fans wanted an official name for it—and that's how flexin' was born. Last time I looked, it's still going on in Boston to this day.

I just love to make a lasting impact.

That moment of doubt from last season, when I was in

WHAT'S DRIVING YOU???

Milwaukee and my leadership was suddenly rejected? I was glad to see that moment was gone for good. I felt like I connected with Doc, with my teammates—and even with the media. I knew how to be engaging and give reporters what they wanted—but I also knew *not* to make it about me. I was about Ubuntu!

Here's how an ESPN article saw it, written during the playoffs:

> *The question posed asked Celtics reserve guard Keyon Dooling about his two second-half 3-pointers that aided Boston's come-from-behind victory in Game 2 of an Eastern Conference quarterfinal series against the Hawks, the first of which snapped a 77-minute, 25-second trifecta-less streak for Boston to start the postseason.*
>
> *Dooling politely tried to steer the conversation to the other end of the floor.*
>
> *"We made some shots, but the key for us was defense," he said. "We really locked in, defensively. We were able to kinda slow [Atlanta point guard Jeff] Teague down—he's like 'The Little Engine That Could,' he's all over the place, but [Celtics guard] Avery [Bradley] did a good job of corralling him, our bigs did a good job of giving us extra shows...It was a defensive win for us."*
>
> *Undeterred, the reporter asked again about the big shots. Keeping with his theme, Dooling got defensive.*
>
> *"No, I heard your question," he said with a smile. "It's not about what I did. It's about our team and our defense."*

263

KEYON L. DOOLING

And there in a nutshell is why coach Doc Rivers loves Dooling.

I guess it was.

As a player, I had a very uneven year, due to some hip and knee injuries. To tell you the truth, the shortened season was very hard on me physically and mentally; it was hard on *all* the players. We had to play a lot more games in a lot shorter window than normal to make up for lost time caused by the lockout. Come March of the season, however, I was taking it to the court again and ended up having some great playoff moments in the postseason.

But my biggest postseason moment ended up happening in the locker room.

It was Game 5 of the Eastern Conference semifinals against the Philadelphia 76ers. So far, the series was tied at 2–2, and at halftime, we were down 50–47. I could tell in the locker room that the guys were a little down and looking for me to say something the way I would before a game to get them feeling strong and positive.

I would do that by looking them in the eyes and saying something like, "I need you guys tonight. Everything you've got, I need it. Listen everybody, we've got a job to do. If your job is to cheer on the bench, I need you cheering! If your job is to play defense, damn it, defend! If your job is to rebound, you'd better rebound! I need you! I'm with you, I'm two feet in and I'll run through a wall right now for you! I'm all in, I don't care about anything else but this team!"

And that was the spirit of what I had to say to them in the locker room that night at halftime. Yes, there was some language that you'd only find in an R-rated movie, but that was necessary to really pump those guys up.

After that halftime talk, we came back and crushed Philadelphia that night, 101-85. After the game, Brandon Bass told the media that the team had received "a sermon from Reverend Dooling" that turned it around.

From then on, that was my name—"The Reverend." Even though I had said a lot of words you wouldn't ever hear in any church, I wanted to raise their spirits just like a preacher and I guess I did just that.

Again, I saw what my true gifts were—and where my future path would take me. It was a sweet time, that Celtics year, my last full year in the NBA. We had a magnificent run; we made it all the way to the Eastern Conference Finals, where we lost Game 7 to my old team, the Heat. They went on to win the championship and good for them.

Being "promoted" to The Reverend was like my graduation from the NBA. It was the culmination of what I had tried to bring to the game, that kind of special energy that would enable everyone to do their best. I didn't have a name to attach to that spirit until I played for Doc Rivers.

Ubuntu. It could truly make the world a better place if we all practiced it.

UP AND DOWN

WHEN THE LOCKOUT ENDED, I was still a Milwaukee Buck. Two weeks later, I was a Celtic. Boston needed a backup for Rajon Rondo, coming off his first All-Star season. I was more than happy to be picked for the job.

The season was over and I was on a high. I thought I was on my way to becoming the person I always knew I could be. Plus, it turned out I was still capable of playing great ball.

Other NBA teams certainly thought so. I had eight or nine other teams offering me better deals than the Celtics. But I remembered when I had left the Heat for a better contract and missed out on being part of a great organization. So I turned down those offers and re-signed at a minimum veteran rate with the Celtics in July of 2012.

It wasn't about money anymore.

What it was about had to do with another special moment for me in the playoffs. Doc Rivers called me out in front of the whole team after we had done badly in a game. Now, I had been called out by Doc before, sometimes in a negative way, sometimes in a positive way, so I didn't know where this was going. But I was happily surprised by what he had to say.

Doc Rivers pointed to me and turned to the rest of the team.

"Damn it, look at him right there. Look at Keyon. Look at him. Look at him! That f—er doesn't care about anything! He's totally given himself to the team. He comes in every day and he does his job with a smile on his face, with heart, with passion. He knows the game plan, he's picking you guys up when you need it! Damn, that's the kind of guys I want to coach. That's what it's going to take for us to win it all. Everybody's got to give everything!"

I wanted to keep giving everything to that kind of coach. I wanted to keep being a Celtic. And I wanted next season to be my finest. During the off-season, I worked out hard. I bulked up. I wanted to be in the best shape of my life and play my best year of bball in the league.

I felt a lot of light. But underneath that light, a lot of darkness was still buried deep inside me. And the dam I had built to hold back that darkness was starting to give way.

I was trying to ignore the fact that, despite my positive feelings about the upcoming season, despite the fact I was motivated to work as hard as possible to make the most of my remaining time with the Celtics, I was completely exhausted. I was tired. I was burned out.

It started with all the stress and the drama of the lockout. Was I going to get paid at all this season? Were all my teammates? What kind of deal would we end up with? Then there was the season itself, shortened yes, but with a whole lot of extra games crammed into the schedule to make up for lost time. Sometimes, we played back-to-back-to-*back* games, something I had never experienced before. Then I also took on the task of being the team's hype man and mentor to those who needed mentoring. It all took its toll. Even the playoffs had a downside—because we had gone so far in the playoffs, the season wasn't done until June, which meant my off-season break would be significantly shorter.

I'm not complaining, because it was an amazing year of growth and achievement. But I could not ignore the fact that I wasn't twenty anymore—hell, I wasn't even *in* my twenties anymore. I was now thirty-two and the average age of an NBA player was five years younger than that. My drive was undeniable, but my equipment was starting to fray; my body was hurting and my spirit was bruised.

That level of exhaustion surely weakened my resistance to the darkness inside me. The darkness that had been there for almost twenty-five years.

The first signs? My thoughts were starting to drift in negative ways. I had always read a lot, but now the stuff I was reading was stirring things up deep inside me. I was speed-reading everything. Yes, I read the Bill of Rights and the Constitution, but I also read the Black Panther Party movement doctrine, I read about the black leader from the early 1900s, Marcus Garvey, and I was dismayed about the conflict between the ideals of America and the reality of life in America.

Then my focus narrowed. I started researching my own personal history. I dug into my ancestry, but I could only trace it back to my great-grandfather. Beyond that? I only knew they were slaves in Gainesville, Florida. That made me question myself. Was that all I was? Did my lineage really dead-end there? Did that somehow make me less than other people?

Now I realize that chasing all that down, my history, my culture, my personal roots, was a lot like chasing the wind. It's certainly interesting and good to know and understand, but it wasn't what I was really after.

No, what I was really after was a way to heal the psychic wound that the sexual abuse had caused. The problem was I just couldn't bring myself to look at it, even after all those years, so I distracted myself with the other stuff. It didn't help. It just brought me closer to the disturbing memories as well as the anger and shame that never really went away.

All that was beginning to bubble to the surface. And one final event that summer would bring it front and center.

There are a lot of different ways to be violated.

As I've mentioned, during the years of my NBA career, I had plenty of people coming at me to try and get a piece of me. People from my past acted like I owed them—and they wanted their payback in money. I was used to that after the initial shock. It happens to almost all NBA players and probably to anyone who achieves our level of success. Still, even though I was used to it, it wasn't fun.

That summer, however, it reached a new low.

One of my best buddies from my pre-NBA days and a family member hit me for a large amount of money. And it didn't stop with me. They also took money from one of my closest NBA player-friends. He was so upset, he shut down our relationship for awhile.

WHAT'S DRIVING YOU???

I was used to bad behavior, but these were people I loved and trusted above many, many others. It was a huge violation and something I never thought could happen.

And yet, the emotions it stirred up were all too familiar. I would get waves of bad feelings and try to compare it to past traumas. I'd end up saying, "Dang, I don't think I've ever felt like this before, have I?" But I knew that I had. And somewhere in the back of my mind, it went back to the molestation. It kept pushing its way up into my thoughts, and I kept trying to push it back down.

It was a struggle I thought I'd win. I thought I *had* won it. I thought I'd be back playing for the Celtics in a few weeks.

But before I went back to Boston, I had to take that trip to Seattle—the trip that would finally force me to deal with my own personal darkness.

THE BREAKDOWN:
PART TEN

RECOVERY

THE STORM HAD PASSED.

From Seattle to L.A. From Boston to the bottom floor. I had been through two weeks of confusion, violence, anxiety, uncertainty, panic, and insanity.

After a very long weekend, I was about to finally find my way out.

Monday rolled around, the paperwork got done, and I was free to leave the mental hospital. I chose not to go to another facility—I knew I couldn't put myself under anyone else's control anymore. Instead, I went straight home, knowing that Doc Rivers and Billy Hunter were working on finding me the right doctor to help me fully recover.

In the meantime, my family had to readjust to who I was—and I had to readjust to them.

There was no question I wasn't the same man. I was following my wife around the house like a lost puppy. If she left the room and went into another one, I went with her. I needed the security of knowing she was right there in case anything else happened to me. The kids, of course, didn't know what to do with me. They weren't used to seeing their dad in that weak of a state.

Meanwhile, I was still acting out. It was still hard for me to eat and I could barely sleep; I got maybe an hour of shut-eye a night. I still felt like I was on a different frequency. I've never been on psychedelic drugs, so I have nothing to compare my experience to, but I was literally seeing things, things I don't even want to talk about because they were too far out.

I interviewed with a couple of doctors in the Boston area to find the right one—and I knew the moment that Dr. Timothy Benson walked into the room that he was the guy. Dr. Benson was a psychologist at Harvard and I connected with him immediately. That was important; I was very vulnerable and I needed to feel like I could trust the guy I was going to work with. I felt like I could trust Dr. B. I told him I didn't know what was going on with me, but I would put myself totally in his hands.

From that moment on, I dedicated myself to the therapy.

But it wasn't Dr. B. that unlocked the first important key to my getting better—it was actually Tosha. She started noticing that, right after I took my meds, I was at my worst. I would start getting agitated and crazy and she saw that the pills, specifically, the blood pressure pill, seemed to trigger my paranoia. Funny how the professionals in that expensive hospital never figured that out.

After consulting with Dr. B., he not only took me off that blood pressure stuff, but he cut the dosage of the other meds by three-quarters. He also got me some sleep medication to help me rest at night.

And working together, he helped me get to the bottom of my pain—and why I had suddenly become so out of control. All those years, since my molestation, I had been fighting different emotional conflicts within me, different insecurities which had begun with my abuse and were aggravated by the enormous pressures put on me by others throughout my NBA career. The betrayal I had experienced the summer before my breakdown broke my heart and opened the psychic floodgates; I could no longer ignore all the negative emotions I had kept in check up until that point, so they overwhelmed me and broke down my hold on reality.

Now, I had to go back to basics in order to regain my mental wellness.

I began that process by doing hour-and-a-half sessions with Dr. Benson, every day, five days a week for my first two weeks of working with him. I took him on a pretty good ride, because, at first, he didn't know who was going to show up for my appointment. Some days I was Tupac, as radical as they come, yelling about "Injustice! Injustice! Injustice! The system! The system!" Some days I was in there like a scared little kid who didn't know what hit him, asking, "Why me? Why me? Why am I going through this?" And then some days, I was just plain lost. I was like, "Where am I? I just don't know, doc." And every day he would try to get to who I really was underneath and build that person back up.

Dr. B. helped me rediscover my own identity and challenged me to find out what I wanted to do with that person. He then gave me the tools to work through all of my pain from the past, from the molestation to the resentment of everyone who had done me wrong; from forgiving myself for mistakes I'd made to understanding what a family structure should be all about.

It was about love, it was about clarity, and it was about putting boundaries in place—boundaries I had never allowed myself to have before.

I not only had to rebuild myself, but I also had to rebuild my family. When you're on the road 120 to 130 days out of the year, it cuts into your family bonds. And my union and charity work had only increased my time away—I just hadn't been home enough in recent years. Now I was there 24/7, except for my therapy sessions—and feeling isolated because I wasn't used to them and they weren't used to me, especially in my current state.

It was time to make some much needed changes, changes that began with allowing Tosha to love me and nurture me in a way I never had been before. After all, I had been the Man of the House—meaning I acted like a tough guy who didn't need that level of love and support. I had to lose that attitude—and let her deep into my heart.

Same with my kids. They knew I still wasn't right, but they were patient and nursed me back. Once that process was done, they started licking their own wounds. We had to do family counseling with them and I had to do marriage counseling with my wife in order to create a new and stronger foundation, a foundation that was built on Christ, strength, love, and respect.

I also worked to restore my physical health. I rode my bike five to ten miles a day, I exercised, and lifted weights. I started doing yoga, and learned breathing techniques that helped me to relax, focus, and feel lighter inside. I prayed, meditated, and centered myself. I bathed with essential oils, which are wonderful therapy for your mind, body, and spirit. I began watching everything I would put in my body and my diet became almost all-natural. I also found quiet spaces in nature where I could relieve stress and gain strength. After a few weeks, I even got off the prescription drugs when I was able to get back into a regular sleeping pattern.

Most importantly, I stayed with my therapy. After the second week of intensive daily sessions, I was able to dial it down to one hour a week. Therapy helped me meet myself; it was the gateway to healing. I embraced the fact that I'm human; I have many emotions and many layers to my personality and I can't hide from any of them. I feel very masculine at times; I feel successful at times; I feel confident at times; and sometimes, I feel insecure. Sad, happy, depressed, doubtful, embarrassed, motivated, encouraged... they all pass through me like they pass through every human being. I accept that. We all have to.

Maybe the most important thing I learned is that, when you really strip away the titles, the blood relations, and the associations from the people in your life, when you really just look at them as you might a stranger, you see they *are* just people—and those closest to you are just as capable of doing bad or good as those you hardly know. And that, in turn, made me realize just how much BS I took through the years.

For awhile, I was mad at myself. I thought I had been too soft, I wanted to help people too much. I just loved people, so why wouldn't I want to? But allowing some of them on my journey (and I'm not just talking about monetarily) took away so much from me. If you spend all your time solving everyone else's problems, you have no time to attend to your own.

That meant I had to go cold turkey. I had to re-evaluate all my relationships and rebuild them from scratch, slowly, with the appropriate boundaries in place. For me, it was empowering—but for those going through that process with me, it was difficult. But I had to do what was best for me and my family. I had to finally get my priorities straight.

My breakdown was over. The rebuilding was in full swing.

REBOUND

SOMEBODY WANTED ME TO PLAY basketball again?

That was one thing I was not even permitting myself to think about. I was busy and I was happy. While I was getting therapy and recovering, the Celtics continued to allow me to work behind the scenes for the team. Again, I can't say enough about how much support this special organization gave me.

My title was player development coordinator and I got to work individually with guys on the court; I got to mentor them, so every morning I would eat breakfast with them, go in the weight room with them, be available for them if they needed anything—just be that big brother. I basically did in the locker room what I always did as a player.

There were also a few new and exciting layers to what I was doing now. For instance, I got to sit in the coaches' meeting and learn Doc Rivers' strategy, so I could communicate that to the players. I also was able to learn from the very top of the Celtics organization, president Danny Ainge. With his approval, I went to every department and asked the people there to share how things worked where they were. I got an invaluable top-to-bottom look at how the business of basketball worked and I ate it up.

My biggest responsibility was my work in the community department; I got to do my speaking presentations. I got to hold the mic and emcee season ticket holder events, elementary school gatherings, and other outreach programs. At many of these, I presented not in my basketball sweats, but in a corporate suit with my Double Windsor tied tight and right. Yeah, I was doing well even with my big boy clothes on.

But, wait. Somebody wanted me to play basketball again? For reals?

It was true. Memphis gave me a call asked if I would consider joining the Grizzlies for the back part of the season, the season I never thought I'd be a part of. They were going to the playoffs and wanted some extra help.

I went straight from the Celtics front office to back on the court in Memphis and I would never do that again. You need three months, maybe four months, to build your body up for a championship run and my body just couldn't handle it. It was too intense. Still, it was fun—it was a challenge I got through and it helped me complete my recovery. It felt like an ending of sorts—and I felt at peace with the fact that I might never play again as a pro.

That turned out to be the case when the 2013-2014 season rolled around. My playing days were indeed over and I officially retired in January of 2014. But I had proven myself one last time with Memphis. That allowed me to walk away from playing the game with my head held high and my heart full of pride.

How do I sum up my NBA career? Well, every player wants to be an All-Star, wants to be a max player, wants to be at the top of the league, and I was no different. However, I ended up hitting none of my career goals as an athlete. As a matter of fact, I failed miserably at all of them.

Does that sound brutal? No, it's just truthful. And besides, I still view my playing career as a successful one. I had to learn to adjust my expectations from expecting to be great to accepting that I was good enough to continue to be valued on the court. And I was good enough to play thirteen years in the league and retire with the respect of many great men that I, in turn, respected.

Sports are very humbling. You either find yourself in sports or you lose yourself in sports; it's a very fine line. My final verdict on myself? I didn't reach my potential as a player—but I exceeded all my expectations as a person. And that's ultimately the true goal.

Being the best person I could be also was the motivating factor behind doing something I had been dead set against—going public about my molestation.

I had wanted to keep that private. As a matter of fact, I wanted to take that secret to the grave. Frankly, I wanted to keep working in a sport that was incredibly guy-centric and I thought this would be a big strike against that happening. Not only that, but I was insecure about how other people would treat me. I was already cautiously rebuilding relationships and was concerned about how this would impact that process.

It was Tosha who turned me around. She said there were a lot of people who went through this kind of ordeal and didn't know what to do about it, just like I had never known what to do about it. She said I had to stand up and make a difference and let other people who had been victimized know they weren't alone.

I couldn't argue with it. I still didn't want to do it— but I did it anyway. I thought I'd just talk about it and it would be over. So I reached out to a few journalists I knew and trusted, gave a few interviews, and suddenly my face was all over the TV and the Internet. Katie Couric even interviewed me on her talk show.

But that was that. I had my fifteen minutes of fame for something I really didn't want to be famous for, and I thought it was over and done. I had to think again. Keyon Dooling, the guy who was burned out from taking care of everybody else's problems, suddenly had more of them on his plate than ever before.

I began to hear from tens of thousands of other victims of abuse, who were reaching out to me to share their stories. And, to my surprise, some of those people were NBA players I was friendly with. They weren't about to go public with it like I did, but they would pull me aside, anxious to talk things over with somebody who understood—and I was there for them, even though I was out there all alone with my story. That was okay, because by this point, my therapy had equipped me to deal with others' burdens being dropped on me. Now, I'm always open and ready for that engagement, just in case I meet some-body who needs to talk about what happened to them. I know how to replenish myself and I know how to go back to my happy place.

However, the stream of people seemed endless—and Tosha again pushed me to kick it up a notch. She said we should do more for all these people—maybe start a foundation and give them resources to help. I was again reluctant to take on this new challenge, but, at the same time, I couldn't help nodding in agreement at her wise words.

This is what I told *The Boston Globe:*

> "...the path I thought I was going to take in this world of basketball, it could potentially come to a halt because I think I have a higher calling to have a bigger impact on humanity. I know I have some work to do out there for humanity.
>
> "It wasn't my choice [to go public]. I was going to do the Katie show and fade to black and focus on basketball and work my way up and maybe become a GM one day and become team president one day. But I can't, when you get hundreds of thousands of people reaching out to you, telling their stories of hurt, kids who can't move on.
>
> "One young man told me he hates telling all his business to the psychiatrist. He hates talking to them. And he told me everything.

KEYON L. DOOLING

"People don't heal. People don't get rehabilitated. People take all this hurt into their adulthood and they keep the generational curses on their family.

"So it's bigger than just me and what I am trying to do. It's about Ubuntu. We need to embrace it."

I did embrace it. And that's how our Respect Foundation came to be.

The Respect Foundation was an important aspect of the overall direction of mentorship and leadership I wanted to go in. I felt my wide range of experiences, as well as the lessons I had learned from those experiences, gave me a unique perspective from which to help others. There was my incredible and exhausting journey from the hood to the NBA, the pressures of that ride as well as the hidden trauma from my molestation, the amazing lessons I had learned from my mentors, and the abilities I had gained through my leadership roles. There was also my access to the secrets of multimillion-dollar businesses as well as the billion-dollar workings of the league, my travels around the world and positive interactions with so many different cultures and incredible personalities and the powerful development of both my public speaking talents and my one-on-one consultation skills.

I had a lot to offer, I was ready to put it out there—and I was already finding a very receptive audience. NBA clubs began to request that I fly in to talk to their high-risk players and do presentations to entire teams.

WHAT'S DRIVING YOU???

Everyone was aware of what I had been through and that I had come through it with flying colors; I was a living success story and they wanted me to help others achieve the same positive results. The NBA was finally recognizing the importance of mental wellness when it came to their players; it was a real issue that had to be dealt with. Owners and players alike saw that I was someone who could make an impact in a positive way.

It was a promising beginning for my post-player career. But I had to figure out how to truly make it a career—how to put a title on what I was doing and continue to make a living.

The title that appealed to me was that of life coach. As always, I went at my new goal hard, taking some courses and getting official certification in the field. And, I developed an overall approach to deliver to my clients.

I realized people's lives aren't about an end goal; it is the steps along the way to a goal that are important (as any fortune cookie will tell you!). Those steps take you to critical intersections where you must face new challenges. The higher you climb, the tougher those challenges become. But if you walk away from those challenges, you don't succeed.

I created a blueprint to help people navigate those intersections—I call it the #KDBluprint—so they can reach that "sweet spot" of personal and professional development and achieve higher levels of physical, mental, and spiritual balance. I do that through a five-step process, which includes:

Discovery: Understanding who you are and renewing your identity

Exploration: Recognizing and managing frustrations and disappointments, facing your past to realize your future, and managing relationships

Balance: Creating disciplines that align with mental health and wellness, and bringing spirituality into your everyday life

Position: Accepting who you are, where you are, and working from that knowledge to develop your own personal blueprint for success

Reflection: Thinking through your personal discoveries and putting your blueprint into action

Since I officially retired from playing, I've acquired corporate clients as well as individual ones. I continue to do speaking engagements as well as work for my Respect Foundation. Now that I'm freed from the pressure and time constraints of my playing days, I have the time and energy to build on the leadership talents that God gave me and my father encouraged.

It's not where I saw myself going when I was back on the neighborhood courts in Fort Lauderdale, but I'm glad I've arrived at this special place. That's the thing about intersections—you never know where they're going to take you.

WHAT'S DRIVING YOU???

There's only one thing that hasn't changed since the old days—and that's the voice I always carry around in my head that's still yelling, "Shoot it, Bubba!"

I always will shoot it, Pop. You made sure I would.

AFTERWORD

POSTGAME NOTES

IN THIS CLOSING SECTION, I want to talk just a little more about how devastating the effects of sexual abuse can be on a child—and why this is a problem that desperately needs continuing attention.

I'm trying to do my part with my Respect Foundation, inspired by my wife, Tosha, which provides support, resources, and information to help ensure the safety of all people regardless of age, race, or sex. You can find out more about Respect at RespectFoundation55.org.

We are believers that sexual abuse can be prevented and, even if a child is victimized, that child can recover. Unfortunately, when that child *doesn't* get the proper treatment, a recovery may never occur.

Because I never dealt with my own pain, my breakdown was gonna happen sooner or later. I've seen all the studies on adult survivors of sexual abuse and that research shows that a lot of us go through physical, biological, and behavioral problems for decades after the abuse happens. Some suffer for their entire lives.

Most ongoing problems stem from the fact that a lot of abuse survivors lose their ability to deal with stress over time; that was most definitely true for me. One study tracked people for twenty-three years after they had been molested as children, and the results showed that they just burn out their body's way of handling anxiety—something scientists call the "stress hormone."

The anxiety that causes this condition comes out of the ongoing worry that kids have after being sexually violated; they can't stop being afraid that it's going to happen again. Victims like me also wonder why *they* were singled out for abuse in the first place. Even if they seem fine on the outside, these kids continue to feel scared and nervous way down deep inside. That constant stress pushes their coping mechanism to the limit, until it finally stops working like it should. In fact, a lot of sexual abuse survivors end up with similar psychological profiles as military vets with PTSD.

My therapist told me I had PTSD for decades and never knew it. Because I never spoke of what happened to me, because I pushed down the anger, shame, and embarrassment I felt because I was molested, I never opened myself up to the healing of my heart and mind. It's like I kept playing on a bad knee and never had a doctor look at what the problem was. That would be crazy—any athlete would know if that messed-up knee isn't looked at, it's eventually going to give in a serious way and the injury is going to wind up being a lot worse than it needed to be.

Sometimes I think that if I had just been able to talk to the right person about what happened to me as a child, maybe what happened to me as an adult could have been prevented. But, again, I was unaware of the danger I was headed toward. After a basketball game, I would ice, I would maybe get a massage, get stretched out, do whatever I felt my body needed. But, until after my breakdown, nobody gave me any clue how to recover mentally when a part of your heart has been shattered. I just didn't have the tools—and to be honest, I had tried my hardest to pretend the whole incident never ever happened.

That's why I encourage any of you reading this book who suffered abuse as a child to seek help if you haven't already. Yeah, you may feel there's no one you can turn to—I felt the same way and, even as an adult, when I finally did reveal my secret, my own family at first did not believe me. Victims are often told they're imagining things.

But you must hold on to your truth, even when others don't believe you. Instead, try to find someone you *can* trust, someone who *will* believe you—and look for other resources in your community that might offer help with your healing.

The biggest mistake you can make is doing nothing because you believe there is nothing to be done. The fact is that negative experiences *can* be overcome, if you're willing to embrace positive solutions. Don't be defined by the bad that happened to you; instead, be defined by the good you can bring into your life.

It's up to you to determine the answer to the question, *"What's driving you?"*

Me, I hope it's a beautiful dream.

A MESSAGE FROM KEYON DOOLING:

Thank you for allowing me to share my story with you! I also hope you enjoyed the art illustration throughout the book, but I didn't stop there. My friend, rapper Bless'ed, and I worked on telling my story through music.

Bless'ed

See the link below to download three (3) complimentary songs from Bless'ed's new album "What's Driving You???"

Please visit:
www.reverbnation.com/theblessedkid

The complete album with all twelve (12) songs is available at iTunes, Amazon, Cdbaby, etc... Thanks and enjoy!